Conquering Your Funk

A Guide to Leading with Your Brilliance and Banishing Your B.S. in Life and Work

By Vanessa C. Newport, SHRM-CP, PHR, GBA

Adam —
Always
lead with
your brilliance!

Vanessa
Newport

Copyright

Brand and product names are trademarks or registered trademarks of their respective owners.

Cover Design: Armejndi

Author's photo courtesy of Joanne Wagner Photography

Advance Praise

"The author helps you find your brilliance and demands that you let it shine. A true guiding light out of the depths of your funk. Vanessa became a bigger advocate for my happiness in the first few chapters of this book than I ever had been for myself in 33 years. I'll change that now!" *Christine O.*

"After reading this book, I understand why I haven't been able to change my situation in the past!" *Brandy J.*

"What a gift we have been offered here. Anyone willing to open their hearts and mind will benefit from this book. Examining ones' self can be painful but powerful exercise, however, reading and applying Vanessa's principles can and will empower you!" *Lori B.*

"Vanessa teaches you how to get to the root of your problem instead of just dancing around it. Her poignant life stories and reliability bring the lessons and information to life. A must read for anyone stuck on the treadmill of life." *Mitch A.*

"Reading this book literally had me exclaiming. 'My life is going to change for the better!' I am known for being a very positive person and I've been working happily with my employer for over a decade, but I couldn't help but find great tools to help me improve in all aspects of my personal and professional life! I have already started a list of loved ones who I KNOW will love benefiting from Vanessa Newport's beautifully honest examples and life lessons!" *Jerrod G.*

"Well written, easy to read book with excellent exercises to examine why you're stuck in your life, how to get unstuck and thus eliminate that which no longer serves you and has been hindering you to be your best, most authentic and happy self." *Barbara F.*

"Understanding how life experiences, including trauma, affects our behavior can be very difficult. Vanessa's book allows the reader to

iv

take the first steps in this process. I would recommend this book to anyone who feels a little lost and wants to develop a plan to move forward." *Bob N.*

"I've always avoided thinking about behaviors that I regret, but eventually you have to deal with your own B.S. and this book teaches you how to deal with it in a unique way using relatable examples along the way." *Kim B.*

"A bold, direct, transparent approach to communicate how self-reflection and discovery led to major breakthroughs, both personally and professionally. This is a smart book with unique stories about how the author found her way through challenging circumstances and is helping others through her experiences." *Vonda M.*

Dedication

To my son, the center of my world.

To my husband, the most patient, trusting partner on the earth, who closed his eyes and jumped with me.

To my mother, my biggest cheerleader.

Table of Contents

Introduction

"No amount of security is worth the suffering of a mediocre life chained to a routine that has killed your dreams." Maya Mendoza

My Story

There came a time in my life when I couldn't ignore the calling anymore. The calling from my body, mind, and spirit that I couldn't continue to do what I had been doing. It hit me so hard that I thought I was dying – and I wasn't even 40. At the very least, I was so miserable that I had a serious discussion with myself about what was going on and the reality of what it all might mean for my future.

As a single teenage mom, my priorities came into focus faster than anyone else I knew at age 19. While my friends went off to college and married their high school sweethearts, I found myself alone with a baby, sitting on the shag-carpeted floor of a double-wide trailer wondering what I was going to do with my life. My destiny appeared to be living there for the next 18 years making minimum wage, and that scared the hell out of me. The "American Dream" seemed impossible to achieve at that point in time. I had, as many people reminded me, already screwed up my promising life by getting pregnant in the first place. That was the second time in my life that I realized my current pain was much stronger than any amount of pain it might take to change.

The first time was two years earlier when I moved out of my childhood home at age 17. I graduated from high school early and began working a full-time job. Technically, I worked three jobs to make ends meet and moved 12 times in the first year. Going back home wasn't an option. My parents' tumultuous relationship was imploding and our small family split apart. I was tired before I added a baby to the mix. But, my work ethic was the driving force for survival and that didn't change when my son was born. Of course, working three jobs was no longer possible simply based on time

1

alone. My expenses versus income were upside down, and I somehow made it through. But, I knew that simply surviving wasn't a good long-term strategy for us. I envisioned what I wanted my future to look like, but it was only through the lens of getting there by a tried-and-true path. The careers I dreamed about having as a teenager were not possible in my new reality.

While working full-time, I started college. My son was six months old. Over the nearly nine years it took me to get my business management degree, student loans racked up. I was rewarded for that hard work and was quickly promoted, over and over again. I threw myself into my job. And it felt good to succeed and be recognized for my hard work and tenacity. But, I never actually referred to my job as a "career." I didn't want to own the fact it was my "career" because it wasn't what I imagined myself doing as a grown up. It was only the path I fell into when I needed a job and continued to get promoted while trying to figure myself out. Before I knew it, I had nearly 20 years of that job, er "career," under my belt. I got the sensible degree; one that I could apply to nearly anything I might want to do in the future – you know, once I actually started living the life I wanted. All the while, my son was growing up, in a house I bought in my early 20's. He took swimming lessons, and played sports like all of the other boys his age. I owned a sensible car and a not-so-sensible car. I dated, trying to find that perfect husband-dad combo.

In my late 20's, I was sexually assaulted at home, by a person in society we are all taught to trust and admire. At the time, I didn't report the crime or go to the hospital. I was just relieved that my son wasn't harmed and that I wasn't beaten or murdered. I excused the situation away, blaming myself for being so stupid and allowing this to happen. I got up the next day, took my son to school and went to work as if nothing traumatic had occurred. Although I talked to a few friends and family about it – they were apathetic. Almost as if they didn't know what to say; people get weird when you tell them about problems they can't fix. Counseling didn't seem like a priority until it was, ten years later.

My house went into foreclosure in the 2008 market crash. By the time the bank finally got around to responding to offers, it was too late. We needed to move to transition my son into a school district that could help with his special learning needs. I could still afford the payments, but my son's education was more important. Sadly, the assumption was made by many that I had made poor financial decisions, resulting in foreclosure. I walked away from that home and started all over again. I can still feel the lump in my throat that I felt when I drove away for the last time. Despite the reason for leaving, I still felt shame associated with the financial ruin I would inevitably cause myself in the process of doing the right thing for my child.

With my annual salary and bonuses, I was earning nearly $100k a year in my 30's. I felt like I had pretty much achieved the "American Dream," and I didn't feel like I really needed a partner to seal the deal. I should have been happy with my accomplishments. By that point, people who had followed my journey for a couple of decades thought I was amazing, especially considering that my transition from a teenager to an adult started out with a huge obstacle. But I wasn't happy. The emotional and spiritual fulfillment was missing despite my professional success. And I wasn't taking care of my physical health either.

I kept pushing forward. My priorities were relatively straight, right? My focus on the career I built, and walking away from my mortgage, was solely based on ensuring that my son's needs were put first. It took me many years later to realize that much of my success was actually a result of having a baby when I was a teenager; he certainly gave me the motivation to ensure I was successful in my career. But, my sole focus on him and his safety and happiness also left me terribly vulnerable in many ways.

Despite promotions and being a technical expert in my field, I struggled at work. On one hand I was respected and valued – my opinions and expertise were appreciated and it felt good to help people with the information I had to share. On the other hand, I was a mess in almost every other way. I wasn't managing in a way that served me, or my team. I wasn't building relationships the way I wanted, and even spent a considerable amount of energy breaking some down. I stopped getting promotions, my performance reviews accurately documented the things I was awesome at, and the things I wasn't so awesome at. The B.S. in my head and heart that had accumulated over my entire life was holding me back in a big way. I was exhausted and needed help, and was too broken to acknowledge it while in the depths of it.

The summer after I turned 39, I experienced the third major physical and mental breakdown I had in 12 years. I had a spreadsheet full of mystery medical problems that I had developed over 20 years and didn't know where to start to fix them. I could barely put my own body weight on my feet and my back, hips, and legs surged with excruciating pain every time I moved. My body movements were strained and tentative, and the limping was obvious. My physical pain was so excruciating that I started using a cane at home. I was too embarrassed to use it at my office, but people noticed something was wrong. My face wore my pain.

I wondered what I did to deserve being so ill. What could possibly be causing this? It was at this point that I realized the pain of staying the same would be worse than any pain it would take to change. We're not just talking about health changes here. My medical problems were really just symptoms of much larger, underlying issues that I needed to deal with. My body finally broke down and aggressively told me that it was no longer acceptable to put everything and everyone before myself. I could no longer push myself and my physical and spiritual well-being to the back burner, waiting for a better time to deal with it. That time was now, and my body wouldn't take no for an answer.

I regretted everything that I had been pushing to the back-burner for so long because it all caught up with me. For a year, I went to more than 100 medical appointments and therapies to try to find healing. It had taken years of internal processing, opening myself up to accepting feedback productively and taking action to change it, counseling and mentoring, and distancing myself from stressful environments to finally start emerging from the dark place I had been in for so long. I realized that my health problems were actually a manifestation of what I hadn't dealt with mentally or spiritually, let alone physically. I was stuck and my body was forcing me to stop and realign my priorities. I literally had to slow down, in order to speed up again. I had to get my head on straight, and start taking action on ALL of the things that really mattered, in order to move forward. I started to develop a plan so that when I was physically able to move forward again, I knew I would move my life in a direction that was in alignment with my heart.

I had done a relatively good job keeping it all together on the surface over the years. I learned from childhood that it's best to keep pushing forward and that working hard would result in achieving the "American Dream." You know, the career, the house, the husband, the kids, the cars, and vacations to magical places. Sound familiar? I also learned that I should be grateful if "the dream" was achieved and I should be happy with what I get. But, as I achieved "the dream," even though it wasn't in a "socially acceptable" order – I wasn't married and was estranged from my son's father – I felt like I was not living the life that I wanted. Don't get me wrong – I appreciated the childhood lesson of survival, but when it came right down to it, it wasn't fulfilling and it was destroying me. Something BIG was missing and terribly broken and now I was at risk for losing more because of poor health. Despite my success, I had to make some new choices.

This was my mid-life enlightenment – it wasn't a crisis at all. Through a thoughtful evaluation of my current life situation, core values and priorities, everything finally came together in my head and my heart. I learned how to frame adversity in a way that was productive, and even became grateful for every hard circumstance I had ever been handed. I learned what my purpose in life was. I learned to open myself up to possibilities and watched them materialize in my life. I significantly improved my health status and

5

pain. I came out of my chronic-depression. I began to appreciate the experience I acquired being in the career I had fallen into, instead of being resentful of it. I actually became excited to live my life with passion. I re-imagined what the "American Dream" could mean for me, with realigned priorities.

I became a new person and started to live the life that I had been waiting to begin for far too long. I recognized my brilliance, and banished the B.S. that had been holding me back.

My journey has led me to the realization that I want to help women like you find a way out of your funk, just as I did for myself. I want to help you recognize *your* brilliance and banish *your* B.S. I want to help you overcome and eliminate the negative thoughts in your head, which lead to unproductive behaviors in life. I want to help you get out of the funk this has caused you for far too long.

Because you're reading this, I know that you also want these things for yourself. You want to turn the "what ifs" into a plan to make it happen this time. You might feel a little, or a lot, broken. You might not know where to start. You might not even know what to ask for. You are likely at a point in your life where you feel like you have so much potential, but something is keeping you stuck. You want to be happy. You are ready to make the changes necessary to transform your life – to start showing up as the person you want to be, to get that job that you keep getting passed over for, to improve your performance reviews, to be the leader that you know is inside of you. And just maybe, you want to serve the world by leading with your brilliance. Like me, you can do all of this by making the choice to take action in alignment with your heart and intentions. And, that's what this book will teach you to do. It will take you through the Conquering Your Funk process that I take my clients through when I am working with them one-on-one, which includes:

- Identifying why you're in a funk
- Recognizing your positive attributes

- Using your weaknesses to your advantage
- Identifying what makes you happy
- Focusing on your future
- Acknowledging your barriers
- Understanding how your perceptions impact you

Lucky for you, I get it. I know you. I am you. I can't want this more than you, but I can want it just as badly for you and walk side-by-side as your mentor.

Head over to my website at https://www.theconfidencespot.com for more information about "The Unfunk Toolkit: 13 Tools to Help Get You Unfunked" which will help you during your journey.

Let's get started, shall we?

Chapter 1 –

What's Got You in a Funk?

"Nobody can go back and start a new beginning, but anyone can start today and make a new ending." Maria Robinson

We all have individual journeys that make us who we are. Some paths are more challenging than others and you may be wondering how the heck you're going to change what's in front of you. You've probably been stuck at this point for quite some time. You're overwhelmed and don't know where to start. I've been there and have uncovered some really important steps that helped me along the way; I'm sure they'll help you, too.

Slow Down to Speed Up

While I'm a huge advocate of focusing on moving forward, we can't start there right now. We will get there, I promise. But if focusing forward is what you typically only do, it's probably the key to what's actually holding you back in the areas you want to change. You're probably moving fast forward on busy work that's actually distracting you from the important stuff, like understanding what's at the root of why you're stuck. That's why I say, you have to "slow down to speed up."

Before we can make any progress looking forward, we have to do some work to look back at where you came from. This exercise can be really hard for those of us with painful memories and experiences. But, I will tell you, getting real about the hard stuff in your head and heart will do wonders for moving you forward and will allow you to get un-stuck.

You need to take the time to answer a lot of deep questions, which "The Unfunk Toolkit" can help you with, such as:

- What were the circumstances surrounding my birth?
- Who influenced me as I grew up?
- What were the values and expectations that were instilled in me by my parents?
- What type of culture was I raised in?
- What was my relationship with my siblings like?
- What were key situations and milestones in my life?

I can't tell you how many counselors I have met whose first question was "So, will you tell me about your childhood?" Have you visited a counselor in the past who asked you to talk about your childhood? Personally, I was royally annoyed when asked this question repeatedly. I wondered why I couldn't just focus on, you know, adult issues - like why I wasn't communicating well with a boyfriend. Of course, there was a reason for this; our childhood significantly influences who we are as adults, and situations we'd rather forget and move on from are silently killing us from the inside out. So, in fact, our adult issues are really childhood issues (i.e. communication problems with a boyfriend stemmed from communication problems in my household growing up). If you can't figure out why you think or act a certain way that is not serving you, chances are it lies in your childhood story – you have a core wound somewhere – something we'll talk more about later in this book. As your life journey continued, you collected more experiences and influences that further impacted where you are today which may be even more challenging than your childhood. As much as you try to push these thoughts off to the side, they swirl, racing in your head. You might feel like you don't know where to begin. For years, I made virtually no progress trying to fix it; I felt like I was getting dragged by a bus. I was in analysis paralysis. There were so many things to fix that I gave up before I even started. You may not even realize how your past relates to your present. You might not think you have the courage to deal with some of the experiences that have impacted you. You are not alone. But I can tell you from experience

9

that it is possible to discover how looking at your past will help you move your future in the direction you want. We'll also talk about all the wonderful things that influenced you (hint, it seems crazy but even negative experiences can actually result in wonderful lessons).

As you're taking the deep dive into analyzing your own journey, you'll uncover that there are five key areas we need to take a deeper look at in order to move forward.

Mental Well-being

What's your relationship with yourself? It needs to be a positive, healthy relationship. If it's not, it's holding you back.

Our World

Have you found a way to help others, with proper boundaries? Do you have a healthy relationship with money? If not, again, that's holding you back.

Relationships

Do you have healthy relationships with those in your tribe? That is, people who you surround yourself with at home, work, and other social activities. Do you know how to communicate your feelings and needs effectively? Are your tribes supportive and encouraging? If not, guess what, that's holding you back.

Personal Habits

Do you have habits that you want to quit, but can't seem to nix no matter what you do? If not, you got it, these are holding you back.

Healthy Living

Are you honoring this one body that you have? Are you taking care of it like the precious resource that it is? If not, yep, that's holding you back too.

So, where do you start with all of this? What if you don't even know if any of these things are holding you back? Maybe you haven't slowed down enough to think about it. Understanding these concepts at a deeper level might seem overwhelming. If they do, don't worry. I'm here to help you discover the answers and solutions throughout this book so we can begin to build your plan for getting you out of your funk. As you're learning, you can only really accomplish this when you get to the root of your current barriers.

Of course, looking back at your journey to this point in your life is only a piece of the process. We also need to uncover other critical components that will be key to discovering your brilliance and your B.S., and get you out of your funk. They include:

What Are You Awesome At?

What have people told you that you are good at? What comes naturally to you? What attributes do others seem to admire about you? This is your light, your brilliance, and it needs to shine!

What Are You Not So Awesome At?

What have people told you that you're not so awesome at? What is hard for you? What do you loathe doing (which often comes across as not being good at)? This is also your brilliance, but is often disguised as your B.S. Your B.S. dims your light, so we need a way to either convert it to brilliance or let it go.

What Makes You REALLY Happy?

What gets you really excited to do and talk about? What makes you feel happy and energized? What lights up your face and body language? This is your brilliance.

What Do You Want Your Future to Look Like?

What do you look like in your future state as you want it to be? Who is with you? How are you spending your time? How do you feel? How do you want to act? What do you want to be recognized for? Are you playing big or keeping yourself small? This is your brilliance intention.

What Are the Barriers to Getting Out Of Your Funk?

Gathering all of this information about yourself is going to be an awesome start to living the life you have put on the back-burner for so long. But, let's get real, you have barriers. You have roadblocks. You have real life happening right now. There are situations that may hold you back. We'll talk about those. The good news is that there are very few situations in life that are going to stay exactly the same. And if there are, we'll figure out how to use those to your advantage. Just keep in mind that you have more control than you think you have right now to make things exactly as you want them to be.

Chances are, you're in a funk because you've been in a boat that's taken you downstream and you don't like the destination – that's because you haven't done a great job of paddling in the right direction. That's ok, you just need to learn how, and that's why I'm here.

This book has been written in a way that can help you understand and implement many of the techniques and shifts in thinking I have used to help me with my own personal breakthroughs.

Chapter 2 –

Unfunk Your Brilliance

"You have brilliance in you, your contribution is valuable, and the art you create is precious. Only you can do, and you must."
Seth Godin

You are awesome at A LOT of things. But, you might not be giving yourself the credit you deserve. There are many reasons that you're shy or maybe even embarrassed about declaring your strengths and successes to the world. It's important to get you more comfortable with this topic, because declaring your personal power is very, well, powerful. It's also the critical foundation from which you can build the future that you want. It's your brilliance and it is what allows you to shine in the world.

Declaring what you're awesome at is one of the most powerful tools that you have in your belt. To skip the process of honoring these is like trying to build a house without the blueprints. You might end up with a house at the end, but it's going to be patched together using materials and tools you happened to collect along the way, and it may not be entirely stable or weatherproof. That would be a ridiculous approach, right? So would ignoring your awesomeness blueprint as you map your way toward your new future.

Stop Being So Damn Humble

I mean it. It's holding you back. Don't worry, I'm not telling you that you should make a crazy list that we're going to later turn into an obnoxious billboard in New York City's Times Square with your face on it. Don't confuse "stop being so damn humble" with being braggadocio. They're two different traits and no one prefers the latter. Your parents may have taught you to be humble and told you to not talk about yourself or your accomplishments. They probably told you how ridiculous you'd sound to other people if you pat yourself on the back, and for God's sake, don't embarrass THEM. Here's the deal: it's okay to talk about what you're good at and to focus on your strengths and successes. And, if you use these to help other people, all of a sudden you are doing a service to people instead of just talking to them about how great you are. It feels a lot better and your parents would be proud.

I used to work with my friend, Melissa. Her office was bare; no pictures or accolades hung on the wall. She even had a master's degree and several certifications, but you would never know it by visiting her office. I asked her one day why she didn't hang her hard-earned accolades on the wall and she began to describe how she was raised to be humble and that earning a college degree was an expectation in her family. She found it uncomfortable and unnecessary to display them; not having them displayed made her feel humble.

My office was the exact opposite. I think I had at least four professionally framed degrees and certifications proudly hanging on my wall. Every time I looked at them, I thought back about the perseverance it took to earn them. I thought about the daily tears that no one saw when I was too tired to read another textbook page or write another essay after a long day at the corporate job and being a single mom. After that conversation with my friend, I felt a little awkward keeping my accolades up on the wall. I worried that she thought I was being braggadocio and that was embarrassing to me. But, she explained that she completely understood why they were important for me to look at every day. And, having them displayed made me feel humble, because I had so much gratitude for the path that allowed me to earn them. They made me feel credible to serve the employees of the company we worked for.

We both had completely different opinions of what made us feel humble and neither of us held on to any judgment for each other about our personal decision. One of us proudly displayed accolades and the other did not, but both of us were in service to others. So, when you're thinking about what your strengths and successes are, if your intention is to be humble and also in service to others, you will not come across to others as braggadocio. It's often others' filters that create labels for us and we hold onto them as truths when they are not. This holds us back.

Human Nature

Your brain is wired to remember the negative stuff (and obsess about it). It's unfortunate, but if you've ever tried to write a list of all of the positives and negatives about yourself, your list about the negatives is probably a lot longer and comes more easily. It's human nature to do this, and frankly, it's a big reason why you're probably stuck. I participated in a Leadership Development program at one point in my career, which included a 360-degree review. This review was sent to twenty of my peers so they could provide feedback about my competencies (or lack thereof). There is no one on the planet that I know who really enjoys getting 360-degree feedback, including me. I had uncontrollable anxiety about this process and gave myself ulcers for months. The leadership program coach attempted to calm me and told me to view the feedback "as a gift." I'm pretty sure I called her some not-so-nice names when I left the room. The survey deadline loomed. All of my peers provided honest feedback. Real, raw, unfiltered, direct, feedback. I cried when I read the summary report and I'm pretty sure I went home early to sulk. I felt like a terrible person. My coach desperately tried to tell me that that report was actually very positive. In fact, there were pages and pages about all of the things I was awesome at. There were relatively few points about things I could do better (and they were biggies) but to be honest, I was already painfully aware of them. And, I hated that I wasn't doing a better job of keeping them a big secret. I felt exposed. I felt like I had been put on notice that all of these people now expected me to change. I didn't want to admit it at the time, but

100% of the feedback in that report was true: all of the positives AND all of the negatives. The negatives hit me hard because I knew that I needed to change them, but I was stuck. I was stuck on all of the things I'm writing about in this book. I needed to change in so many ways to start showing up in life differently, but I didn't know where to start and I was not doing a great job of keeping that a secret anymore. My peers knew I was unhappy and it was manifesting itself in a not-so-productive way at work. This is when my second breakdown occurred; I needed out and I found a new job. I took the review folder home and stashed it in a cabinet.

For six months, I kept running into the folder. Every time I did, panic set in. My breathing got shallow, my head spun with all of the thoughts about what I needed to change, and my stomach churned in knots. I wanted to shred that document so badly, but I didn't even want to touch it. So, I left it in the drawer.

Another six months passed and I decided to shred the document. I didn't need all of that negativity in my life! But, I read it one last time as I tore each page from the spiral notebook with the intention of feeding it to the shredder. As I read, I thought, "Wow, I *am* pretty good at that!" and "Yes! I love doing that!" and "I am totally the expert in that!" and the other truthful feedback about the stuff I needed to change didn't sting like it used to. I had already implemented steps to improve the constructive feedback that was written on those pages and feeling really good about it. It was that moment I recognized that I was leading with my brilliance and banishing my B.S. I collected the torn pages, which had been saved from the shredder, and filed them in the drawer again.

Wherever You Go, There You Are

This shouldn't be surprising, but the new job didn't solve all of my problems. The job wasn't really the problem, it was me. When I left, the problems followed. I needed to find solutions for areas I was struggling with. It was at this point that I really started developing my own process of showing up in life the way I wanted everyone to see me. I pulled the torn pages of the 360-degree review out of the cabinet and started diving in, without the battle gear on this time.

Can you relate? If so, you might be finding yourself wanting to constantly change your environment in hopes of your world drastically changing. Sometimes that is absolutely the answer – like if your personal safety is in danger, or you're told to do something illegal – and sometimes the answer lies within yourself.

Start Your List

As you begin to think of your list of strengths and successes, I encourage you to make a list of the positives first. Don't allow any negatives to enter your mind and don't write them down if you do. You should bask in the glory of your awesomeness; in your brilliance. I want you to look at that list and think "Damn! I have some gifts to share with the world!"

Think about the following questions to generate ideas:

- What makes you feel proud?
- What comes easy for you that others seem to struggle with?
- What do others ask you for help with because you are the expert or trust your opinion?
- What awards or achievements have you accomplished?
- What has been written about you in your performance reviews?
- What does your family say about you?
- What do your friends say about you?
- What do social groups say about you?
- What knowledge, skills, and abilities do you list on your resume?
- What are your hidden talents that you haven't shown the world yet?

Head over to my website, https://www.theconfidencespot.com/, for a "What Are You Awesome At?" worksheet, which is part of

"The Unfunk Toolkit: 13 Tools to Help Get You Unfunked" and will help you during your journey.

Unfunk Your Brilliance

Chances are you haven't taken any quiet time to think about it, you're being too humble, or you're letting the negative thoughts outweigh the positives. All of these are barriers and are holding you back. If you really can't figure it out, sit down with a friend, or a supportive significant other and they will help you uncover many things that you may not even realize about yourself. In fact, I'm a fan of posting a brief message on social media or email asking for feedback.

Something like the following may allow you to start creating your list:

"Friends/Family, I'm asking for your help with a personal development program that I am working on to better understand my strengths and successes. Because all of you have different perceptions of me, I would appreciate any candid feedback that you would share with me about what you think makes me awesome and what my gifts to the world are. I am very interested in finding out what others think about me that I may not already be aware of. Please post here or send me a private message with your thoughts. Thank you in advance!"

Your list will start growing immediately. Your friends and family will love to tell you how brilliant you are, and you should take it to heart. The list you create will be foundational for your brilliant leadership, both personally and professionally.

Chapter 3 –

Unfunk Your Weaknesses

"My strength and my weakness are twins in the same womb."
Marge Piercy

You knew this was coming, right?

Yep, if you're going to make a list of all of the things you're awesome at, we also need to make a list of the things you're not so awesome at. Yes, this is a lesson in self-awareness and it can be really hard to come to terms with the truth (remember my 360-degree performance review story?) But, I want you to write this laundry list so you can get it out of your head, learn the lesson, AND THEN MOVE ON. That's right; I'm giving you permission to just stop obsessing about all of the things you're not good at. There is no way every person on the planet is good at everything, so just know that you're awesome at certain things that others are not and vice versa. Expecting yourself to be a "master of everything" is like going to the zoo and expecting elephants to climb trees. That's ridiculous! Yes! It is. Make a mental note of that every time you give yourself a hard time for not being good at something or knowing everything there is to know. In this chapter, we're going to learn that once we see our weaknesses as precious information that we can learn from, we can use it to our advantage. Weaknesses don't need to be a place where we get stuck and keep us playing small; they should not dim our brilliant lights.

What Elmo Taught Me

I remember the first Easter with my son. He was five months old and I had just turned 20. I literally had no money in my bank account; it was probably negative to be quite honest. Needless to say, our first Easter was humble. Of course, my baby didn't care either way. It was another day of eating, sleeping, and you know, diaper changing for me. But, I still wanted to do the American-Dream-perfect-mom-thing and buy him a stuffed bunny at the very least, but I couldn't afford it. He did get a stuffed toy; however, it wasn't from me. My mom bought him a Tickle-Me-Elmo stuffed toy that day and I was crushed. I didn't even want him to have it because I wanted to be the first person to buy it for him. I wanted to be the first person to do everything for him. I was too prideful. I felt like I was failing at this single-mom thing. I didn't allow the joy of having a giggling stuffed toy into our home because I was resentful. I was mad at my mom. I was mad at Elmo. And he lived in a box on the top shelf in the bedroom closet.

Of course, this issue wasn't about Easter, my mom, or Elmo. It was just my B.S. – my ego – getting in the way. Unfortunately, it took me over a decade to realize this. My ego made me too proud to have someone else help solve a problem for me; it sucked the joy out of the spirit of the gift. This was not an isolated situation for me; it became a really integral part of my personality and it didn't serve me well.

Before reading further, stop and think for a moment. Do you have an Elmo in your life? The sooner that you can get out of your own way and allow others to help you during times where a weakness or failure is presenting itself, the faster you will be able to move forward. Sometimes your brilliance shines, and sometimes the brilliance of others needs to shine in order to help you when you're stuck.

Why Weaknesses Are Actually Awesome

A weakness is simply something you need help with. Maybe you want to get better at something that you consider a weakness or maybe you don't. Either way, if a particular skill, need for knowledge or ability is critical to your future success you will either need to get help to improve it or hire someone else to do it. If you have the time and interest, then by all means, hire someone to help you improve whatever skill is lacking. But, sometimes it's just better to spend your energy on what you're already good at, and you should just hire someone to do it for you. It's a short-cut; save yourself time and hassle when it makes sense. For example, I love web design. I kind of wish I would have learned to code way back when. I enjoy the technical and creative process of creating websites. However, if I spent time now trying to be the world's best webmaster, I wouldn't be using my brilliance. In fact, I would be avoiding doing what I was actually good at doing. It's just not a very good use of my time and I should really just hire someone to do it for me. This is why your weaknesses are awesome; it allows others to shine with *their* brilliance!

The caveat here is that you can't outsource everything you don't have the time or interest in. If you want to exercise more, or improve your relationships, or find God, you can certainly hire a mentor like me to help you with your journey, but you still have to do the work. If you say that you don't have the time or interest for the things you can't outsource, you're really just making the choice to not consider it important enough to work on. It's always your choice to do or not to do something and to accept the consequences that go along with it.

Failures Are the BEST!

It's human nature to feel terrible and beat up when we fail at something. We've disappointed ourselves and possibly others who expected more from us. We live in a time of perfectionism. We strive to have a perfect home, to be the perfect worker, be the perfect

PTA mom, and don't even get me started about looking in the mirror. Bleh. Being perfect is flipping boring, although I admit that I used to spend a whole helluva lot of time trying to be perfect. Even Thomas Edison, the holder of 2,332 patented inventions, knew how awesome failures were when he said "I have not failed. I have just found 10,000 ways it did not work." Do you know how much information you have after failing? Oodles. You have oodles and oodles of information and that is awesome. Use that information to move forward but please don't let it hold you back anymore. Perfection in all respects is an unattainable standard; give yourself a break.

Getting Out of Your Own Way

This might sound like it's really hard to do! It might take some practice, but you can do it! Your ability to frame weaknesses and failures in a productive way is 100% up to you. You can't pay anyone to do this piece for you. You have to deliberately choose to think this way. Even if you have a non-productive thought, you can actually stop in the moment and reframe the situation in your head to think about it positively. That is, until it just becomes natural to think differently. Speaking from experience, it has been absolutely empowering to stop beating myself up for everything I don't know, everything I'm not good at, and putting up barriers to receiving others' help. And it can be empowering for you, too.

Your Future Depends on You

Even if you haven't spent a ton of time envisioning what your future self and plan looks like, I guarantee getting out of your funk doesn't include living in an environment where you're surrounded by all of the things you're not awesome at. Will it include a wall of awards of everything you're not good at? No. Will you have a bunch of stories about how your ego prevented you from achieving your goals because you wouldn't accept help from others when you needed it? Of course, not! You won't have room in your new story for all of that ridiculousness. You only have room for the positive

23

things you create, so why spend your time in the present focused there?

It's Okay; It's Just Your Amygdala Screwing with You

I'm not one of those people who goes around telling myself or others that "thinking positively" will zap all of the negative thinking out of your head. Change is deeper than that and frankly, it's not that simple. Your brain is too amazingly complicated to insult it that way. It's actually biologically designed to think about the negatives in order to avoid danger and protect you. So, if it doesn't feel easy for you to reframe negatives into positives, that is completely expected. You are literally going to be trying to reprogram something that has been in your genes since the dawn of humankind! If you're interested in learning more, do some reading about the amygdala – that part of the brain that records and stores the negative stuff. I like to think of myself as a bit more modern than the way this ancient programming had me thinking and that requires absolute practice and intention.

Think about when you learned to ride a bike. Before you started, you may have thought you couldn't do it and were afraid to try. When you got the courage, and hopped on for the first time, you probably didn't ride all the way around the block. I wasn't with you at the time, but I bet your experience was similar to mine: I started, stopped, and fell about a thousand times. I ran into the curb and over the curb and to this day I still don't like riding through sand. And, who was there helping you? A coach. A mentor. Maybe it was a parent or a sibling or the neighbor lady. But you had to work on improving your balance and confidence with absolute practice and intention, and your coach was there to help support you. In your head, you eventually started telling yourself that you could do it because you were doing it, and continued to get better and better over time. Replacing your negative thoughts with productive thoughts can be just like riding a bike.

24

Start Your List

So, let's write your list. It will feel so good to get all of these annoying little nags out of your head and on paper. Then, think about why you might be holding that attribute as something you think you're not awesome at. Now, is this your thought or was it placed there by judgment placed by someone else? What are you gaining from this situation? Does that belief serve you? Why do you think you think that way? How could you benefit by not thinking that way? Is it possible for you to start doing the thing that you're not so awesome at, in a way that serves you? What's the potential correlating lesson?

Let's take my ego/Elmo example from earlier and walk through how I thought about these questions to reframe a negative into a positive:

1. I'm not-so-awesome at: Accepting help from others.
2. Why do I think this? I have pushed people away who have tried to help me and have demonstrated lack of gratitude.
3. Is this what I think or did someone plant this thought? No one planted the thought, I am not good at accepting help from others.
4. What am I gaining by thinking this? I suppose I think that I am showing others that I can handle things myself and be independent.
5. Does that belief serve you? Not really, I could use the help! I am getting nothing out of thinking this way. I don't even feel better.
6. Why do you think you think that way? I have made some mistakes, like becoming a mom when I was a teenager, so it's not others' responsibility to help me with the problems I created.
7. How could you benefit by not thinking this way? It would sure take a lot of stress off my shoulders if I just asked for help sometimes.

8. Is it possible for you to start doing the thing that you're not so awesome at, in a way that serves you? Yes! I think I can start asking for help sometimes when I need it the most.
9. What might be the lesson in the thing you're not-so-awesome at? Well, maybe I need to trust people more. I need to trust that they love me and want to help me no matter what, and that I shouldn't feel guilty for asking for help.

See how I did that? I turned this not-so-awesome thing into a positive way to approach it in nine steps.

Your list of perceived weaknesses might look like this:

- I am too shy to talk to strangers
- I am not a good writer
- I suck at doing math in my head
- I am not a good manager
- I am too fat to have my picture taken
- I have never been able to share my opinions openly
- I won't ever be able to pass that important test
- I can't earn more than what my current paycheck is
- I am not smart enough to start my own business
- I am too scared to take public transportation
- I am too soft-spoken
- I am terrible at being organized
- I can't multi-task

Let's walk through another example; here's the situation: You were promoted about a year ago, into a management position. You had never been a manager before, and although you were excited for this next step in your career you felt that you weren't really prepared (this is the way it usually happens, by the way). Your new company hasn't provided any leadership training. You're screwing things up with your employees and you don't feel very good about the position you're in. You're wondering if you're going to get fired if your employees provide feedback that they aren't happy with your management skills. You don't think you're a good manager.

26

Here's how to reframe that negative into a positive:

1. I'm not-so-awesome at: Being a good manager.
2. Why do I think this? First, I feel uneasy about being a manager. I am nervous. Also, feedback I have received from my boss and my 360-degree performance review says that my team does not think I am a good manager.
3. Is this what I think or did someone plant this thought? Both. I think this about myself and I am being told this.
4. What am I gaining by thinking this? Nothing. I continue to act like I am not a good manager because people think I am not a good manager and I feel like I am not doing a great job. I am going in circles.
5. Does that belief serve you? No, continually thinking that I am not a good manager is not making me be a better manager.
6. Why do you think you think that way? I didn't really get any training on how to be a manager, let alone how to be a good one. I was promoted because I was good at my job, but I have never led people before. I was just thrown in there. I feel like a fraud.
7. How could you benefit by not thinking this way? I would probably be more open to learning how to be a good manager. Right now I am so stuck on how I am not good that it consumes my confidence.
8. Is it possible for you start doing the thing that you're not so awesome at, in a way that serves you? Yes! I can start thinking about this differently. I can start acting the way I think a good manager would act, and I can go to my boss and let them know I could benefit from some formal management training.
9. What might be the lesson in the thing you're not-so-awesome at? Well, maybe this is a lesson that I need to advocate for myself more, in order to be in service of others. I would not have been promoted if my boss didn't see potential in me. And, my boss knew that I didn't have formal management training when I was promoted into the position. Perhaps they are waiting for me to demonstrate leadership skills by asking

for help in an area I am weak and they will appreciate my initiative.

Now you try it. Get the "Reframing Negatives to Positives" worksheet from my website, https://www.theconfidencespot.com/, which is part of "The Unfunk Toolkit: 13 Tools to Help Get You Unfunked" and will help you during your journey.

After working with my client Sarah on her weaknesses using the reframing process she said "I was totally able to see how it was possible to change the way I was interacting with people in public. I have never been very good at making eye contact or chatting, but I was able to see how that wasn't helping me grow my business. I was in a funk because I didn't have the confidence to talk to strangers and I was afraid I was going to fail. After working the process and realizing that it wasn't helping me to stay stuck, I feel a lot better approaching people and I have already made some new sales!"

Unfunk Your Weaknesses

It's really important to acknowledge what you're not-so-awesome at because it gives you more information to work with in a productive way. Can you imagine how you will feel when you turn all of the not-so-awesomes into pure brilliance? We want to incorporate everything you're brilliant and awesome at into your future state, right? So, when you write a list, there is just one rule: for every negative you list, you must perform the nine-step process to understand how you can frame it to serve you.

If you get stuck here, get the "What Are You Not So Awesome At" worksheet from my website, https://www.theconfidencespot.com/. You guessed it - it's another free worksheet as part of "The Unfunk Toolkit."

Above all, remember that you're awesome at a lot – and you'll be even more awesome after you convert every weakness to a strength. This process will help you get out of your funk.

Chapter 4 –

Unfunk Your Happiness

"Why do we only rest in peace? Why don't we live in peace too?"
Unknown

Sometimes we spend too much time looking around for happiness. Even waiting for it to drop out of the sky. I know that I did. We ask ourselves questions like: Where is it? Is it under this rock? Is it behind that door? Will a new job create happiness? Would I be happy if I lost 10 pounds? Wouldn't I be the happiest person on earth if Adam asked me to marry him? Can't Kelly see that if she changed her ways we would all be happy? But, aren't we missing out on happiness right now – in the moment – when we're just sitting around waiting for it to magically appear? Or, maybe even more challenging than magic, waiting for other people to change? Or, running away from the B.S. we think is preventing happiness when we have the power to fix it all along? Or, not stopping to smell the proverbial rose?

I say yes! We are missing out!

I didn't allow myself to feel happiness in my life for years. I pushed the pause button. I got all serious. It's not like happy situations weren't surrounding me at all times, it's just that I did a poor job of allowing myself to feel it or to intentionally create environments where happiness thrived. I kind of revolted against happiness. I acted like reserving my happiness for later was some type of great commodity-preservation strategy. I remember telling a counselor one time that even if I won the lottery, I wasn't sure I would be happy about it. He looked at me like I was crazy. I suppose deep down I felt like I didn't deserve to be happy. I hadn't checked all of the things off the list yet that I thought would magically open the gate to happiness. But, all of those life shaping events continued happening and still affecting me at my core. And, I was letting all of that stuff about what I wasn't awesome at, tear away at my confidence. Why would the universe want me to be happy? I mean, look at all of this drama in my life. I wasn't enjoying the journey. I was waiting for the destination before claiming happiness. The problem is, in life the only true end destination is death and then it's too late to share your happiness with those you spent your life with.

Man, waiting to feel happiness was a drag. I was so stuck in my B.S. and it was holding me back from living the life I wanted. After many years of mentoring and counseling, the light bulb went on. I came to acknowledge that happiness is abundant! I don't need to conserve it or wait for it to happen to me to feel it. I can make happiness happen RIGHT NOW! The universe wants me to be happy, and create happiness – and the more of that I practiced, the more of it I got! Don't get me wrong, I didn't immunize myself from the shit-storms of life, but I felt so much better about the potential outcome while in them! Regardless of my circumstances, I had the choice to be happy. And, so do you.

Now, let's imagine a two-day charity bike ride in the Rockies. There are three classifications of people who participate:

- Type 1: Those who over-prepare, show up too early, and start riding before the race begins, finish early
- Type 2: Those who prepare, start with everyone else in their wave, finish among new friends
- Type 3: Those who have not prepared, start whenever, lag behind

Type 1 finishers are focused on the destination. They have the top of the line bikes, they have their nutrition all figured out, they blast through rest stops, they don't make new friends, and they're done with the race before the Day 2 finish line party has begun. Then, they are pissed when only a water station and a vacant port-a-potty greet them. They wonder, "Where are all of the people cheering me on? Doesn't make me feel very awesome about being first."

Type 2 finishers are focused on the journey. They have their bikes figured out, they know they will be taken care of if they need pickle juice or energy drinks, they stop at all of the rest stops and listen to the band, eat BBQ dinners, and make new friends. They start Day 2 with their new friends – their newest cheering committee. They reach the finish line hand-in-hand with new BFFs. They think, "Wow! Look at this party thrown for me! I feel like such a winner!"

Type 3 finishers are also focused on the journey, but may never finish. They show up for a mountain ride with a beach cruiser. They wear jean shorts and forget their sunglasses. They didn't train and they struggle. They make friends at the rest stop, but are consumed by thoughts of quitting. They may or may not start Day 2 with the new people they've met. If they're lucky to cross the finish line they aren't even paying attention to the party. They think "This sucks! I am never doing that again!" And then they sign up for next year's event and again, don't bother to prepare.

As you live your life, which type of person are you showing up as? Do you show up the same way in both your personal and work life?

Sadly, I showed up as a Type 1 finisher in much of my career, with a bit of Type 3 tossed in there. I desperately wanted to be a Type 2 finisher, but I was stuck in my B.S.

Feeling happiness and showing up as the type of finisher you want to be is powerful. It's like a free drug, without any nasty side effects, except possibly for a few people who will judge you for being all chipper as they secretly wonder what prescription your doctor put you on. I don't say this lightly. I have been on more anti-depressant prescriptions than fingers and toes on my body. But, I gave up. I grew tired of the guess and check process, trying to figure out the type and dosage, and not knowing what symptoms were related to what. Going to the doctor every six weeks to check in along with the roller coaster of feelings in between (or not feeling any progress at all) was draining and expensive. After a while, I didn't have the stamina to figure out if something could really help and it certainly wasn't convenient to go to all of those medical appointments. Add to that, an incorrect diagnosis and corresponding medication regimen in the middle of all of it made me wonder if I was losing my mind. Truthfully, none of those medications made me feel better than when I just started changing my thinking in an intentional way – and it was a fight. I acknowledge that anti-depressants may be critical for you. I have absolutely no judgment either way. I just hope your journey of finding something that worked for you was better than mine.

Regardless of being on medication or not, MAGIC happens when you connect your livelihood to a happy state of mind, feelings, and situations. Your brilliance can shine brighter than you ever thought possible. Conversely, it is not possible for your true brilliance to shine when you are not happy. And so, your light is dimmed and your awesomeness cannot be seen by those you are called to serve because they are blinded by your B.S.

Do me a favor, well for yourself really, and sit quietly and think about something that makes you happy. I mean REALLY happy. Maybe it's puppies. Maybe it's seeing one of your kids do something amazing. Maybe it's something you accomplished that you feel proud of. What does the physical sensation of happiness feel like to you? Start from the top of your head and work down to your toes, evaluating each part of your body as you scan down acknowledging how happiness makes you feel. Take long, deep breaths as you scan through each part of your body, evaluating your feelings. Close your eyes for a moment and do this.

Now, evaluate if your life and work is aligned with this level of happiness feeling. Your life needs to make you feel like you're surrounded in a room with a bunch of puppies (or whatever makes you happy) every moment of every day. And if it doesn't you have the power to change that. For those of you shaking your head "no" right now, I really mean it. You are responsible for the path you are creating for yourself every single day. You are responsible for the thoughts in your head that make it so.

The Sensation of Happiness

About fifteen years ago, my son and I were exiting the highway and stopped at a red light. A homeless man was standing at the side of the road peering blankly into my car. He had the prettiest piercing blue eyes; the same color as my son. I think most people missed seeing that about him, with his dirty, torn clothing, and overgrown gray eyebrows. He was stoic. He wasn't even holding a sign. It was obvious that he would take anything offered. But, I didn't have anything to give. The feeling of not helping made me feel terrible. My heart was heavy as I drove home and my mind raced about what I could do to help. It was then that I decided to make some care packages. My five-year-old son helped and we drove around scouting for people to hand them to.

During that drive, I went back to the intersection where I saw the man who inspired me to do something that made me feel happy. He was there. I pulled up and handed him a care package out of the car window. It included snacks, toiletries, a winter scarf and gloves, and a Christmas card with a simple message of hope and peace. I don't think I had ever seen anyone's eyes open as big as his did that day. He didn't even smile. He was in shock... like a kid on Christmas morning. He snatched the offering, a bottle of water, and limped away quickly, hiding the bag in his jacket so no one would see his loot. Time stood still; my memories of this moment are in slow-motion. Seeing how happy he was made me happy. And watching my son observe that exchange made me happy. REALLY happy. That feeling in my heart is what I want to feel all of the time.

Recalling that story brings back the physical sensations I had back then as I handed the care package out of the window. My brain feels like it's buzzing, my eyebrows are lifted, my sinuses are open, my eyes are burning and swelling up with tears, I am smiling, my chest is rising and falling as my breaths get faster and deeper, my heart burns and beats hard in my chest, my stomach is fluttery, my legs and arms are jittery, my toes wiggle... this is how happiness makes me feel.

The job I went back to the next day didn't make me feel this way. In fact, it was sucking the life out of me. I cried. A lot. And I continued my journey of trying to figure out how to connect that feeling of happiness with Monday mornings.

What Does Happiness Look and Feel Like to You?

I would like you to really understand what happiness is to you, as it's the fuel to allow you to show up the way you want to be seen every day. When you think about what makes you happy, what are you doing in that moment? Who are you with? What is your intention? What does it feel like? How often do you allow yourself to feel happy? This is a great exercise to get clarity about what makes you feel good.

Try to spend a week documenting all of your happiness experiences. I mean those that make you REALLY happy. Make a list to reflect on.

You can also think back to your childhood and teenage years. What did you enjoy doing? Imagine yourself as a child, observe what you were doing and evaluate if it made you happy. If you stopped doing it, why? Can you start doing it again today.

Guess what? Other people know what makes you happy. Just ask them. I bet you can get a really long list of observations that other people have. Sometimes when we spend too much time in our own heads, we don't even see simple or obvious answers. This exercise goes along really well with asking others for feedback about what you're good at, too.

And, when you get to talking, I mean really talking, what gets you fired up? I'm not talking about gossip (that's part of your B.S.). But, what can you just talk non-stop about to your BFF? What makes your energy shift and people start to listen? What gives you all of those happiness feelings? Add these ideas to the list of what makes you happy.

Waiting to Feel Happy

When you take a look at your list from the week, consider how many of those situations were happen-chance, in-the-moment surprises. And how many of those were situations that you put in motion because you knew they would result in something that would make you happy? By setting intentional plans to make yourself happy, you have so much control of getting out of the funk you're in! Don't wait to feel happy, friends, create circumstances where you expect happiness as an outcome on a constant basis. This is how you look forward to experiencing life.

Your Career Happiness

We spend so much of our time at our jobs, doesn't it make sense to do what makes us feel the best? Sometimes we fall into something and travel down a path for a long time and it treats us pretty well. So, we keep doing it. But at the end of the day, we still end up asking ourselves if we just spent the last 10 hours doing the things that made us REALLY happy. If you can answer "Yes" to this, you have found the secret sauce to aligning what makes you REALLY happy with "work." If you answered no, we have some work to do!

There is a way to align both, and it takes patience, dedication, and a plan to getting there. Sometimes you don't have an idea or a plan; you just feel that you're not in the right place or you're not doing something right. You know you have a gap in a skill set, but maybe you're not confident enough to declare it or faking it until you make it. You might feel like a fish out of water. The exercises in this book can help you get more clear with what's in your head and heart.

35

Happiness Trolls

These are people who want to suck the life out of your happiness. They aren't happy, they are annoyed that you're happy, and they'll do anything to squash your happiness. I've been around a lot of happiness trolls in my life, and it even turned me in to one for a while until I broke free.

My teenage years were tumultuous at home; going to school was actually a relief and I practically lived there. I had just rebounded from a bout of mononucleosis, which I swear stole brain cells and made me sleep for months. I don't remember a whole lot from my junior year of high school, to be quite honest. Sometimes I looked at my best friend and could not, for the life of me, remember her name. But, I do recall a day that I was feeling REALLY happy. It was game day, so I had my cheerleading uniform on, bouncing through study hall with a skip in my step and no cares on my mind – a totally rare experience. I probably had a new love interest and a good hair day. And I got a part in a school musical which I was super excited about. I'm sure I could have ruled the world that day. I felt like a normal 17-year-old for a moment. But only for a moment. From across the room, the study hall advisor, who was also the mother of one of my peers, shouted across the room "Miss Vanessa, you need to get your snooty-ass-nose out of the air right now!" The world stopped. The words echoed in the room and 200 of my peers stopped what they were doing and stared silently at both of us. I stopped bouncing. I stopped smiling. I put my chin to my chest and quickly found a place to sit. No one talked to me at the table. I felt so exposed. I stopped feeling like a normal 17-year-old. Those words crushed me. She had no idea the power that it took for me to feel that good in that one moment in time. She had no idea of the power those words would still have on a woman 20 years later. Sometimes, when I find myself feeling REALLY happy, those words still spring into my head, along with all of the terrible feelings of shame and embarrassment associated with that moment. That's my B.S.

It's taken a lot of practice to re-train my brain, but that damn amygdala likes to hang on. Chances are, you have had some Happiness Trolls in your life too. They start to make you think that your happiness is not important and in fact, something you should feel ashamed about. You shy away from happiness because you associate it with a stupid situation when you were 17 that no one else on the entire freaking earth remembers except for you.

Consider who is in your circle of influence. This is your tribe. These are your peeps. Are these people supportive of your desire to change or the future you want to create? This is a really important question, because answering no can keep you in your funk. You may need to change your circle of influence to pull in others who share your same goals, and create some boundaries for those happiness trolls. Your tribe has great influence on moving you forward or holding you back.

I understand that it's hard to get the ridiculous programming out of your head that trolls planted there; it seems impossible at times. And, I've needed mentors along the way to help me learn how to not allow the trolls to run my life from the negative deep programming of my brain. It's still hard. But I've learned that it was about the troll's unhappiness – it was about their B.S. – not mine. And, I was giving it a whole lot of real estate in my head and heart.

Unfunk Your Happiness

You guessed it; you really do have to unfunk your happiness for your brilliance to shine. Set your intentions positively and step into being happy as a choice. I want to live my life every moment surrounded by the people who make me happy, doing the things that make me happy, using my skills and strengths that make me happy, in every hour of every day. And, I bet you do too.

Yes, there are certainly things that we do that are not our favorite (like paying taxes, and cleaning the cat box) but if you're spending most of your day on things other than those that make you happy, you'll probably continue to be in a funk. Let's change that!

Simply put, unfunking your happiness is all about managing your own thoughts; reprogramming what your default thinking is.

After working with my client Megan on unfunking her happiness, she sent me the following message "I realized that my family members were major happiness trolls! I hate to admit it, because we are so close, but every time I got excited about starting something new they had something critical to say about it. They weren't being supportive at all. Vanessa helped me figure out how to communicate with my family about my goals, as well as some boundaries around myself so I could continue to move forward, despite the trolling!" If it worked for Megan, imagine what it can do for you.

Chapter 5 –

Unfunk Your Future

"You control your future, your destiny. What you think about comes about. By recording your dreams and goals on paper, you set in motion the process of becoming the person you most want to be. Put your future in good hands -- your own." Mark Victor Hansen

Do you find yourself saying things in your head like, "I wish I could do that!" or "I wish I could be that!" and then follow- it up with "Someday..." or "What am I thinking... that's not possible for me." You're not alone. That was totally me. Sure, I have accomplished a lot of things in my life, but there were so many more wishes and dreams inside my heart and I was sure they were out of reach.

Looking back, there were tons of brilliant experiences I wanted in life; highlights included:

- Astronaut Camp. Do you know how badly I wanted to go to astronaut camp at Kennedy Space Center in Florida as a kid?
- I wanted to be a comedian on Saturday Night Live (SNL). My childhood friend and I would put on some badass living room shows. Man, her parents had some patience – and they really laughed (even if we sucked).
- I wanted to act and sing on cruise ships and travel the world. And, of course eventually end up on Broadway, duh.

Did I achieve any of these? No. Why? It's quite simple.

1. I didn't intentionally set a path toward achieving them.

2. I let the B.S. in my head talk me out of thinking I was good enough to be or do any of these things in my late teens and early 20's.

I Got in My Own Way

I ran across a brochure when I was a kid about astronaut camp. To be honest, I think I just wanted to leave the earth and perhaps find solace on another planet, or universe, like many teens. But, at the very least it would be really cool to say I went to the moon, even if it was virtually. I didn't even ask my parents how we could make this work. I didn't think about finding a way to save money to make it happen. I just kept dreaming about how amazing this would be, and all of the reasons why it wasn't for me. First of all, I was a girl. Girls don't really do this type of thing. I have to become a scientist? I don't think I'm smart enough for that. I don't even know if I am going to college. Anyway... my parents don't have that kind of money and asking them would stress my hard-working mother out. SCRATCH THAT. A girl can dream though, right?

When I am in my element, I am actually really hilarious (or at least I think so and that's all that really matters). I discovered that attribute when I was in elementary school. I have always been able to make people laugh, and have quick come backs and like to make people chuckle. I loved reenacting SNL. Loved it. But, life was serious growing up and it seemed disrespectful to "my situation" to be comedic and happy. I didn't find things funny over time and I funneled my humor into sarcasm, and I learned that there is only a special crowd who appreciates that. I was hurting and I wasn't really all that funny anymore. I figured that I was no longer the ideal candidate for SNL and scratched that off the list too.

Everyone thinks they can sing like a Broadway star in their shower, and I was no different. I did some middle- and high-school productions, and even community theater as an adult. But in the tiny window between graduating from high school and going out into the big bad world, thought about considering this as a possibility. You

40

read that right. That's about as far as it went. I was sure I would suck at auditions, that I would be too embarrassed to be any good. Also, it might be too scary to leave home and live on a cruise ship when it came right down to it.

Did you pick up on the trends in my stories? Yep, I didn't work a plan to achieve my dreams and I let my B.S. be bigger than me, BEFORE I even had collected any facts. I pre-judged. Hell, maybe NASA was trying to fulfill a goal to get more girls in their program. Maybe SNL needed a sarcastic actor and would have allowed the path for me to find my authentic self. Maybe I was the next breakout star for a cruise ship line and could have moved to Australia as my new home base. Maybe.

What Happened Instead

Life. Life took me where it wanted because I was not making deliberate choices aligned with where I thought I wanted to go. Even if I had started in one direction and I decided it wasn't for me, it would have been better than not making any decisions. One thing is for sure, life keeps moving forward, even if you're stuck. It will pull you downstream wherever it wants when you're in the boat, but not controlling the direction.

You do this when you are overwhelmed and don't know where to start, and when you are escaping something where anything seems better than where you are. And then 20 years pass. And while you may have made other deliberate choices along the way, they were more aligned with your new reality than what your heart wanted you to do.

As a teenage mom, there was no cruise ship career in my near future, no Broadway, and no going to the moon. While I did make the choice to have a baby, I didn't deliberately choose it. My lack of making other intentional decisions allowed me to be pulled downstream. I wasn't in control of my boat. Before my epiphany about my purpose in life, I wondered how different life would be if I

41

didn't have my son when I did. And, I realized that he was placed on my path to lead me to my ultimate dream, which is helping you. The universe was very intentional about this, even though I didn't see it as such for nearly 20 years.

And, do you know what I still want to do deep down?

- Go to the moon
- Be on SNL
- Be in a Broadway show
- Perform on a cruise ship

And, I think these are all possible now. But, my dreams shifted over time, and other ideas have replaced them as priorities. If I wanted to pursue them, I know there is a path to get there. I just have to create a plan and be intentional about the steps I need to take to get there.

Lorne Michaels, call me. You can really make all of my dreams come true in one quick skit.

Your Intentional Future

When you think about what you wanted your future to be, do you still have those dreams? Or have they evolved into something else? Maybe a little of both? It's okay if you don't know. Life can make us get stuck and funky. I was in such a whirlwind, focusing on the chaos of the moment (for at least a decade) that I didn't spend a lot of time getting back on track and pursuing who and what I wanted to be. Chances are, you've spent a lot of time on other well-placed priorities too and now you're in a funk.

Beyond what you think you might want in your future state, how do you want to feel? Think about what you want to be doing and close your eyes and feel what it would feel like to be in that place. Do you imagine yourself failing at that dream because of your head talk? Do you think about all of the things that have held you back so far? No! You imagined yourself being successful in your future state. You imagined yourself wearing what you would be wearing, living where you want to be living, with the people you want to be with. You just envisioned success. You were able to envision success because you changed your thoughts, for a moment, about possibilities.

When I lost my house to foreclosure in 2008, it was a huge hit to my confidence. It was the first home I bought – in my early 20's – and I was so proud that I made that happen for my son. I knew walking away would really screw up my credit and I was sure I wouldn't be able to ever buy another house again. I mean, who would give me another mortgage when I didn't follow through with my promise about this one? Life moved forward and after one apartment rental, and renting a home from a friend, my son and I moved into my boyfriend's townhouse on the opposite side of Denver. I liked the new town, and I liked living with my boyfriend, but it wasn't *my* place. The energy was all out of sorts and it only allowed in a tiny bit of sunlight in the afternoon. It drained me. It made me sad. And, it didn't have a yard for my dogs. This didn't feel like home. Because of the foreclosure and other debts I had accumulated, I felt trapped. I thought that there was no way we were going to able to move for decades because we were in a hole. But, time passed, and I considered the possibility of making it work. I set my intention on making it work. I learned some great techniques for paying off debt and more time passed. Every month, I evaluated what our debt situation was and what it would take to move. I started asking questions to realtors and mortgage brokers and became really knowledgeable about the selling and buying process. I kept my boyfriend-now-husband updated with the progress, and at one point I told him that we were ready – we could start looking for a new place that was bigger, had a yard for the dogs, and was energetically uplifting. We started our search and signed a contract for a new home, which took 11 months to build. From the time of the foreclosure until the new home was purchased, 7 years had passed. But I had done it. I set the intention, created a plan, monitored it, deliberately worked it, and made it happen.

Getting Really Clear about Your Intentional Future

It's great to take a minute to visualize a possible future state, but it's not very comprehensive. You might have a lot of ideas about what you want to do and how you want to show up in life, but haven't pinned it down. That's ok. Your ideas might change over time, but you really have to start taking action to make stuff happen. Dreaming gets you nowhere except being annoyed that nothing is happening.

In order to get really clear about your future, you'll have to spend time committing to visualizing all of the possibilities and all of the details that can make you smell it, feel it, taste it, hear it, and BE it. You've already done the work clarifying what you're awesome at, and what makes you excited. You already know that you have some work to do in your head and heart to make your desired future a reality. And, let's assume for this exercise that you have mastered and melded all of those things together. Now, you are ready to start writing down all of your ideas about your intentional future (don't worry, you will FOR SURE be adding and modifying this throughout the process).

As you're writing ideas about your intentional future state, answer questions like:

- How do you look? What does your hair look like? What clothing are you wearing? What does your body look like? Do you look relaxed? Do you look excited? Are you smiling?
- How do you feel? Are you REALLY happy? Do you feel confident? Do you feel like you are in your element? Do you feel on top of the world?
- What are your thoughts? Are you thinking about how awesome you are? Are you funneling your energy into what you're not good at? Are you feeling super confident?

44

- Who are you with? Which people are surrounding you? Who are you spending time with? Are these people supporting you? Are you serving these people with your awesomeness? Is this your current tribe, or new people, or a mix? How do those people look?

Get the "Envision Your Future" worksheet from my website at https://www.theconfidencespot.com/, which is part of "The Unfunk Toolkit: 13 Tools to Help Get You Unfunked" and will help you during your journey.

The Stuff You're Afraid to Envision

When I started this process, there were things I was afraid to write down. I was playing small in my head. I was okay declaring things that I thought were pretty possible, but not the things I really truly wanted to make happen. I didn't want people to think I was nuts or impractical. And, could I REALLY do those things anyway? That was my B.S. thinking again. Many of the people in your current tribe are probably used to playing small. That's ok; it's what we're programmed to do. They might encourage you to dream big, but not that big, because, you know, life and reality. That's holding you back.

Go ahead, write it ALL down. ALL OF IT. You will thank yourself for not thinking small anymore. And guess, what, YOU CAN HAVE IT. Look in the mirror and declare something you want for yourself. Then look back at yourself in the mirror and say "Self, you can have it." Make a daily ritual out of reading your intentions, telling yourself you can have it and adding more specificity and desires each day.

My mentoring students get the opportunity to declare their intentions to me, and I tell them they can have it. It's very powerful.

The Magic in Declaring It

Here's the deal. When you put intentions out into the universe, magic starts to happen: GOOD AND BAD. So, when you're writing your intentions down, this energy goes out and it comes back to you. I used to think this was kind of hokey. Eh, someone telling me to just think positively? I am in the middle of real life here, with real things going on, really serious things. I don't have time to sit around thinking positively. You know what I got? More of sitting around not thinking positively. So, if you're sitting around talking about all of the bad things happening in your life and things you wish you could change, you are sending out the energy of those same things to keep happening and you'll keep wishing things would change. If you do the opposite, which is talk about the good things happening as if you have already experienced them in that way, as well as the things you want to attract into your life, you will attract more of those things. The most amazing thing about this is that you have the absolute power to draw the awesome things in just by putting your energy there intentionally. This is 100% in your power, and who doesn't love that? You may have heard of this practice, called manifestation or The Law of Attraction. I had unknowingly been practicing the Law of Attraction all along. I was getting a lot of stuff related to what I wanted to change and a little of the stuff I was getting which is EXACTLY where my energy was focused.

Let's practice. Say you go to a car dealership to purchase a new car. You know exactly what features you want and your budget is $25,000. As you sit down to discuss your dream car with the dealer, you start saying this:

- Rear-wheel drive is ridiculous. Um, no. I live in a snowy climate and I won't be able to get to work. It's $5,000? Ok, toss that in.

46

- A cassette player? No way. Who uses those anymore? I recycled all of those tapes ten years ago. It costs $1,000 to add it? Let's do it.
- Leather interior? I don't want that. I have dogs. That will get screwed up big time. I mean, their claws will shred the hell out of the seats, the car will look terrible, and when I trade it in I won't be able to get top dollar. $3,000? Sign me up.

Do you see what is happening here? You're using up your car budget on all of the things you don't want because that is where your focus is. By the time you start talking about what you do want, you're out of money. The more you think about what you don't want, what you hate, and what is stupid, the more you are asking for getting things you don't want, what you hate, and what is stupid.

Lack of Intention in the Workplace

When you aren't leading with intention, your default programming is reactionary. You're not directing where your boat goes. Are you one of those people who are constantly running around like crazy people hopping from one thing to the next without having set an intentional plan for the day? If you don't intentionally plan it, you are giving up the direction your day takes you. Yes, things come up, I get it. But if you're not leading with intention on most days, you're living in a reactionary world.

The reactionary world can be unnerving. You don't know what kind of shit is going to be thrown at you, and you have little emotional capacity to deal with it logically. We can then make bad decisions and fret over them all night long. This world also leads to lack of making decisions. The overwhelming feeling takes over and paralyzes the decision-making process. And, we all know how unhelpful that is.

When we're not leading with intention, we're probably not able to lead others effectively either. How many times have you seen a manager who is out of control, putting their battle shields up as they go throughout their day in an attempt to deal with craziness? They're in the ditch and not guiding the direction that the ditch is being dug. They are not proactive. They don't recognize the small things going on around them that really matters. Maybe you are that manager? When you're in this headspace, you can't serve others. We are only serving ourselves under the cloak of helping others. Everyone sees through this shit. I know it, because it was on my 360-degree performance review.

Are you leading with intention or reaction?

Unfunk Your Future

Your thoughts are the currency of what you want to bring into your life. Both good and bad. You can change how your currency is spent, starting right this very moment by being intentional about how you choose to spend your thoughts. Manifesting what your intentional future looks like is critical to moving forward and getting out of your funk. Sure, you might want different things now for yourself than what you wanted as a kid and that is absolutely, perfectly wonderful. But, you need to have a pretty good idea about the direction you want to go so you can create an actionable plan to get there. Remember, without a plan the river pulls you downstream when you're in the boat, but not controlling the direction.

This is the difference between dreaming about things happening and setting an intention for something to happen. Whether the intention is in your head, said to the universe, or directly to others, accountability is immediately introduced into the equation. Dreams don't require accountability, but intentions do.

Starting this very practice was absolutely key in changing the trajectory of my life. Once I was deliberate in my practice, my brilliance started to shine, because I was spending my time calling it into action. And, my B.S. was easier to forget because I chose to no longer spend my currency on it. I started attracting awesomeness, and was better able to manage obstacles, simply by how I chose to start thinking.

My mentoring students learn how to apply different strategies for manifestation and intention and if you're thinking this concept is hokey, it's holding you back.

My friend Robin's Story

Owner, Rojo Leather Handbags, https://rojoleather.com/

Although she has a career that others dream about, she knew her corporate VP of Marketing job wasn't entirely serving her heart's passion. So, she decided to take action and elevate her hobby for making luxury leather handbags in her basement to the mainstream fashion industry. Her "passion project" as she calls it, was open for business within one year from the time she set her intention to go for it. All the while working her full-time corporate job and raising a large family. The process of finding production partners, importing leather, designing and approving samples, and figuring out what products and colors to launch was really challenging -- especially in light of delays which moved her target launch date -- a big deal in the fashion industry where getting the right product and colors to consumers at the right time can make or break your business. "I'm living out my own personal brand through this business – I have control over every part of the customer lifecycle which is important to me," she boasted. Robin's corporate job has provided her the opportunity to work with wonderful clients, and income and stability to pursue her passion. She doesn't know what the future holds for her handbag business, but her sales are hitting the mark since launch and she is planning for next season's line of handbags now. "I know of three people right now who really want to start working on their own 'passion projects' to move their life in another direction. The only difference between us is that I started taking action to make my dream happen."

Chapter 6 –

Unfunk Your Barriers

"I am not what happened to me. I am what I choose to become."
Carl Jung

Ah, one of my favorite topics. Barriers, all of the reasons to stay in a funk. They are so easy to list and to keep doing, and then also be pissed off about because they keep us stuck. I was a pro at letting barriers keep me playing small for much of my life. My perceived barriers kept me in an insane head space. I felt like I was in that movie *Groundhog Day* from 1993 where Bill Murray kept living the same day over and over until he got it right. Of course, I had breakthrough accomplishments (they are on my personal awesome-list), but that list had the potential of being much bigger, much sooner, had I found a way to plow through the B.S. that was holding me back.

Barriers dim your light and keep you from being brilliant and feed off FEAR: False Evidence Appearing Real.

However,

- Barriers do not translate to impossibility
- Barriers do not mean we are not meant to do something
- Barriers are not telling us we shouldn't go for it
- Barriers are not telling us it is not worth the challenge of attaining a goal
- Barriers do not mean it's too hard

What if I told you that fear is just a made-up emotion and that you were completely responsible for feeling it or not? Would you be fearful of not being able to be afraid? Ask yourself what you are getting by being afraid of something. Is that fear serving you? What are the REAL risks of what you're afraid of? Sometimes thoughts of fear don't even come from us. It's someone else's B.S. they projected on us and we accepted it as truth and it then became our B.S. Many of us let fear paralyze us, which prevents us from stepping into our brilliance.

Fears can be planted in our minds by our parents, who are just trying to protect us from the big bad world. My mom was raised in a small town and has lived a fairly simple life. She was raised to believe that working a respectable job, having a good work ethic, and being a rule follower were critical to a good life. And, she instilled those qualities in me. None of those are bad qualities to have. But, they also came with the messaging that living outside this box was scary. It was too risky to do unconventional things. That I might end up in trouble, or fired, in jail, or even dead if I broke the rules. And that might be terrible, and embarrassing, and would certainly screw my life up. Yes, all of those things could be true. But all those things could also not be true. My mom's programming became my programming, which influenced how I lived my life, and resulted in my being fearful of opportunities and prevented me from finding a way around barriers that I told myself were unreasonable to consider. These fears were unproven and unnecessarily held me back from making bold decisions that I knew were my calling. It's not my mom's fault, it's just how parental programming works. When I raised my son, I did the same thing. And, now that he's emerging as a young adult, I'm trying to reverse a lot of the programming I instilled in him. The jury's out on this one.

We all can get stuck with B.S. stories – either our own or those planted there by someone else – that prevent us from taking action on possibilities. Sometimes it's just easier to give up when faced with pushback and go where the river pulls us. Perceived barriers also prevent us from doing the type of work we want to do, or being the employee that we want to be, or the leader that we imagine ourselves being. This is how we end up in the wrong jobs or acting in a way that is not in alignment with our integrity. It's much easier to take the paved flat road instead of creating a path through the mountains. These keep us in a funk.

Core Wounds

Earlier, I mentioned the idea about a core wound, typically one defining moment in our past that allows us to get stuck in some B.S. that profoundly influences our experience in the world from that point forward. This wound kills your spirit. When you recall it, you can literally feel your heart breaking back in time. Sadly, if you don't acknowledge the wound and work toward resolving the pain it caused, it can keep you stuck forever.

When I was in second grade, my dad introduced my mom and me to our new neighbors. He had been hassling me about something stupid, as per his M.O., and I was bawling. My face was red and puffy and I couldn't catch my breath. It wasn't the best time to meet new people. He proceeded to introduce me as "the cry baby of the family" and laughed, as tears continued to stream down my face. I could see the neighbors' hearts break through their facial expressions when they looked at me with compassion.

After that, I avoided crying in front of anyone for decades. I held it inside – especially in front of my dad. It slipped every once in a while. But, mostly I ran away to my room and hid, and cried whenever I needed to. I have always been a highly sensitive person, so I cried – a lot. I didn't like this label. It made me feel bad for showing my emotions. It made me feel vulnerable. And, I never trusted him with my feelings again. The path of dimming my light and hiding my brilliance began. Self-defeating language accumulated in my head and destructive habits, like binge eating and starving myself, were planted. This led to a life of hiding much of the time, so I would not be seen being my authentic self.

As a result of this one point in time, I realized my core wound, is "Not Being Seen." And the universe absolutely accommodated my thinking. I played small, I didn't advocate for myself in times that I should have – like when the parents of the kids I babysat decided who was the least drunk to drive me home. I didn't say anything as a kid when the family friend's older brother French kissed me – he was 20 years older. I never told my parents when my crotch was grabbed by a classmate in middle school or when the creepy neighbor hugged me romantically and put his tongue in my ear. I never reported the sexual assault I experienced in my 20's. I never thought people really wanted to see me, or my emotions. And as an adult when I would get skipped over in line at the grocery store I would literally say to myself "Am I invisible or what?" I didn't want to be seen and the universe cloaked my energy in vibration with my thinking. Core wounds are a BIG deal.

Please, please, please do me a favor and get help dealing with your core wound. It does not have to define you. It does not have to make you small. It is NOT you! It is something that happened to you that influenced how you dealt with other experiences later. You are bigger than that situation and you were born to shine your brilliance, just like me.

Barriers Galore

Anything can be perceived as a barrier if we want it to, but that's not serving us, right? When we spend our currency on barriers, we don't have enough to spend on possibilities – the stuff we actually want. But, before we can start thinking about barriers differently, we have to get real. There are legitimate barriers, and some of them may be impossible to get around directly. However, there are usually alternative paths that can be considered as an indirect or alternative route.

So far, we've briefly talked about the following that may be holding you back:

- Your life story
- The list of what you're not awesome at
- The fear of using what you are awesome at to serve the world
- Your health status
- Strained or broken relationships
- Bad habits
- Circle of influence
- Negative thinking
- Lack of happiness
- B.S. stories
- Lack of clarity
- Lack of taking action
- Your damn amygdala
- False perceptions
- Bad assumptions
- Parental programming

Now, let's take a deeper dive into some other potential barriers.

Mental Well-being: Trauma You Haven't Dealt With

Trauma has a profound impact on how we interact in the world – how we perceive ourselves and our worth to those around us. It changes us, our spirit, and our path. We view the world through a lens that we think no one understands. Our personalities change, our physical appearance changes, our communication style changes. We become cynical and full of fear. It's a destructive path to self-preservation – we can really screw things up because the world doesn't understand why we're doing what we're doing. And sometimes we don't either.

One of the most profound traumas I experienced was being sexually assaulted in my own home in my late 20's. I didn't realize the full impact though, for over ten years. I hadn't made the connection that the extreme changes I was experiencing were a direct result of not getting help from a professional.

I didn't report it to the police, I didn't go to the hospital. I took a shower. I cleaned up my ransacked house before my son woke up. I got up the next day "like normal" and took my son to school and went to work. I felt disgusting and dirty. I felt ridiculous that I allowed this to happen to me. I felt like I got conned into letting this man into my life because of his respectable job. I felt like I would be judged for not keeping my son safer. I didn't want to be revictimized by the legal process. I didn't feel safe anymore. I considered buying a gun. I looked over my shoulder everywhere I went. I avoided driving through the cities where he worked and lived. I changed my appearance by gaining a lot of weight and dressing in an unflattering way. My heart became hard. I had trouble trusting people. I closed off my circle of friends and became distant.

I tried to talk to a few people about it early on. But, their reaction was awkward. They didn't know what to say or how to act, and the subject was changed like we had been talking about the weather. I didn't talk to a counselor for over ten years about it, but I had two major mental and physical breakdowns in the meantime. It was just so much to handle on top of trying to be the superhero, single mom, and climb the corporate ladder.

You might imagine how all of this translated into my job. It wasn't entirely pretty. I took on an over-bearing, fighting, masculine energy. I mean, I was winning awards for my work, but my 360-degree review was a glaring reflection of all of the B.S. I was bringing to my workplace. That was my wakeup call that I needed to start working through it and how it affected me. It was controlling my life and I wanted it back.

The mentoring and counseling I finally received allowed me to see the blessing in the trauma, to have gratitude for the opportunity to share my story and help others. I learned that I had a choice to let it continue to control my life, or to use the experience to help other women identify how trauma may be impacting their lives in ways they may not even realize. I chose the latter; unresolved trauma held me back

What traumas have you experienced that may be a barrier holding you back? Are you ready to get counseling and mentoring to help you discover your brilliance again?

Our World: Your Money Shit

They say it's the root of all evil, but I don't believe that. Money is an awesome exchange of energy that allows the universe to keep moving. I didn't always think this, however.

We get most of our beliefs about money from the families we grew up in. I grew up with a "scarcity" mindset about money. If I needed more money, I was taught to just go get another job. Hence, the reason for juggling three jobs straight out of high school. A scarcity mindset makes us think that we never have the money, or we will never have the money, or there is no way to get the money. We are always in "I'm poor" mode. There is a major difference between being poor and having cash flow challenges.

I learned to disconnect from a lot of my money shit over time. It's only money. I've always pushed the boundaries. I maxed out credit cards and paid them off. I trashed my credit score and brought it back again. My house was foreclosed on and I bought another one seven years later with my husband. No matter what money situation I have been in, I have always recovered. There is always a way around the barrier.

Now, it didn't mean that this process was painless for me. It was the total opposite of that. Having creditors deliver lawsuit papers during parties isn't fun. But, it didn't kill me. Hiring a fraudulent debt-consolidation program that was supposed to help me and hiring an attorney to start a class-action lawsuit wasn't fun. And, I recovered. I've listed a resource in the back of this book if you want to learn more about dealing with your money shit.

Your mindset about money may be holding you back with the work you are doing. If you are undervaluing yourself, or letting someone else put the price tag on your time and value, you have some money shit. If you do not believe firmly in your value, you will not get paid what you deserve. If you cannot convince yourself of your worth, you sure as hell won't be able to influence anyone else.

Thoughts can be money shit too – the currency in your head, influencing everything you do and say. I talked earlier about how spending all of your thought currency on things you didn't want, was going to leave you without the things you do want. Don't waste your precious thought currency on anything other than what you desire. It's not worth the high cost of living the life that you don't want and attracting all of the crap into your life that you really want to get away from.

Money shit, in paper and thought form, will hold you back. What's your money shit? And, how is it serving you?

Relationships: Projecting Your Own B.S. on Others

I used to work with a woman I really liked. I mean, really. She was nice, and friendly, and really good at her job. She seemed to let stress roll off her back and was easy going. You'd think I would have tried to make friends, right? Nope. I was mad at her. I was mad at her because she reminded me of someone I had unresolved issues with. I projected all of my relationship B.S. with another person on her. She was confused and I don't blame her. She asked me why I was so angry and I couldn't answer her. I know I wasn't supportive of some personal decisions she was making, and how I thought they might affect me personally, and that was very real. But, I personalized her decisions way too much. They reminded me of how I was impacted earlier in life with a similar situation. Our relationship was broken for years, but when I finally realized what I was doing and had a heart to heart with her and we were able to

58

move past my bad behavior. But, my behavior held me back for years.

Are past experiences impacting how you are treating other people? Are you acting out in a non-productive way?

Personal Habits: Changing Your Ways

Old habits are so hard to break. And, you know this. But mastering this is CRITICAL to getting out of your funk. If you keep doing the same thing over and over, you'll stay in a funk. You have to make decisions intentionally different going forward. They say it takes at least 21 days to make something a new habit – either starting something new, or stopping something old. Just sticking to 21 days can be really challenging, but it is possible if you are connected to why you want to make the change.

I like to set large goals, which I call Macro Goals, and then set smaller goals, which I call Micro Goals, every 21 days. This process helps reinforce new deliberate changes I'm making, without making me feel like I have to achieve the goal overnight. I think that we tend to not stick to goals because we're trying to accomplish too much at one time. We didn't gain 50 pounds in one day, so why are we expecting to lose it in one day? Our society does a pretty good job of delivering instant gratification on so much; we are not realistic about our expectations.

Here's an example about how to set Macro and Micro goals: Say you smoke 7 cigarettes per day and your goal is to quit altogether. Today, just commit to smoke 6 cigarettes per day for 21 days. On day 22, reduce to 5 cigarettes per day, and so on. If you slip up, simply stay on the Micro goal that you're having trouble with for another round until you master it, then start reducing again. You can apply this to things you want to start doing more of as well, such as drinking more water or exercising. The sky is the limit with ideas this will work for. I'm excited to share that I am working with an App development company to bring a tool called "MORPH: Change

Your Habits, Morph Your Life" to the smart phone market in 2017, to help you with your Macro and Micro goals.

What habits would you like to change that would improve your life? What can you commit to start changing your life today? Make a heart connection to the reason you want to make this change.

Healthy Living: Advocate for Yourself

I was relatively healthy growing up, despite a bout of mono in high school. But, I would not be so lucky in my 20's and 30's. Over time, I developed a long list of medical problems which I organized into a spreadsheet in hopes of my physicians being able to see a clear connection and easy solution to my problems. That didn't work. In fact, the more organized I got, the more intimidated my doctors got. I tried to find new traditional western health care professionals who wanted to look at the whole picture. Nope. My spreadsheet was folded up and placed in my medical file. This reminded me why I let my health spiral out of control. Most doctors I had gone to over the last 20 years felt like a barrier, and I just didn't have the energy to advocate for myself the way I needed to. I let this barrier defeat me.

It wasn't until my health wakeup call when I was 39 that I realized that I had no choice but to advocate for myself, hard. It was either that or die a slow miserable death. Self-advocacy lead me to over 100 medical and therapy visits, which included western medicine doctors, rheumatologists, neurologists, pain specialists, physical therapists, emergency room visits, functional medicine doctors, mental health providers, chiropractors, acupuncturists, and massage therapists. I joined a gym with a pool and hired a personal trainer. Every visit was more information I collected about myself and my path to healing, and it was FRUSTRATING. I spent more than $20,000 in out-of-pocket expenses trying to heal what I pushed to the back burner for 20 years. I am not out of the woods, and I don't know if I will ever feel 100%, but I feel much better. I wish I would have taken action sooner; I lost so many years being sick and tired and frankly, took my health for granted and it held me back.

How well are you taking care of yourself? What can you do to advocate for your health?

Tipping the Scale

All of us depend on a variety of coping strategies to deal with our problems. Some of those strategies can be extremely helpful and productive, but can also get us into an even bigger funk if we're not careful. Several of my personal coping strategies turned into bigger problems for me:

- Cleaning
    - Pros: I worked off excessive energy and my house was spotless!
    - Cons: Obsessing over vacuum lines in the carpet was not productive and prevented me from dealing with the real issues causing my excessive energy and anxiety, such as the unresolved trauma I experienced as a child.
- Eating
    - Pros: After years of eating very little to prevent the cruelty of teasing from peers, eating food on a regular basis was a good habit to start.
    - Cons: Eating excessive amounts of food to deal with depression, heartache, sexual assault, and general lack of self-love, didn't actually result in me getting help for any of these situations and left me in an even bigger funk as I fought with managing my weight for nearly two decades.
- Pet Collecting
    - Pros: The power of having pets as companions cannot be overstated. Having dogs during my childhood prevented me from running away from home and gave me something to hold on to when I felt like I was losing everything I had.
    - Cons: Caring for nine pets at the same time, all while being a single mom obsessed with cleaning, became overwhelming and unmanageable. Someone in my family called me a "pet hoarder". Ouch. At some point, the

unconditional love that I received by all of my furry friends turned into resentment, and a feeling of being trapped and guilty for spreading my attention too thin. Having more pets didn't get me closer to a feeling of stability and unconditional love. I just had more to be in a funk about as I was overwhelmed with self-imposed care-taking responsibilities.

What types of things do you use as coping mechanisms? Have they tipped the scale from being helpful and productive to causing you added funk?

Barriers are Breakthroughs Waiting to Happen

Just thinking about all of these barriers is enough to make the average person want to quit. You think that maybe these barriers are messages from the Universe that you are on the wrong path. That you should quit. That it's a sign that you should turn back. It's quite the opposite, really. Barriers are just a sign that you're about ready to make a major breakthrough. Think about a NASA space shuttle. When it reaches a certain part of the atmosphere, it endures massive resistance and must break through the barrier that has been keeping it safe and secure. Once the barrier is breached, it is in outer space, where anything seems like a possibility.

You're not the average person. You're brilliant. You're the person who's ready to make some bold changes. You want your brilliance to shine and to show the world who you want to be. You want to lose the B.S. that's holding you back. And, you want this today.

My friend Peggy's Story

Owner, Peggy Willms Consulting, LLC, https://www.facebook.com/peggywillmsconsulting/

"I have trucked through decades in the health and wellness field as a business owner, personal trainer, medical office manager, and most recently a transformation coach for an extreme weight loss boot camp program. I felt an internal battle daily working in an environment driven by someone else's belief system and their core values. My passion, ethics, and integrity became less and less aligned. My desire has always been to make an impact generationally (to depths) -- not just follow protocols or only touch lives at a superficial level, gather a buck, and ask, 'Who is next?' It was horrible but beautiful timing when my answer came. My adult son was involved in an accident which left him unable to care for himself for a long period of recovery. During this down time, I was able to face my own wounds. I made a list of what I wanted and didn't want, personally and professionally, and soon I realized I would be back working for myself again, coaching a smaller group of clients to ensure quality with desired flexibility to travel, and to live near the sun and beach. Within three months of his healing, I had completed it all." Peggy lives by the motto "authenticity or the highway" and walks her talk. Her biggest fear is having to fill out an application to work in corporate America again, which is the best motivator to make her independent gig thrive.

Chapter 7 –

Unfunk Your Perceptions

"I've always loved butterflies, because they remind us that it's never too late to transform ourselves." Drew Barrymore

In Too Deep

Sometimes when we're in the depths of a major funk, we get the answers we're looking for, and we still don't feel like we have any. We're swirling – we don't know where to start. We don't know how our current realities will give us the space to change, to make room for the new. So, we stay right where we are because at the very least, we know where that is. We know what to expect from that place. And it's that very place we hate to be.

If your reality seems like too strong of a force to allow you to start making changes, I would encourage you to change your perception about possibilities. Just moving your thoughts and actions in an intentional way towards what you want and how you want things to be, will start to change them. Your realities are giving you the very strength that you are seeking to transform your existence. Your realities will propel you forward, even though it feels like they may be holding you back. I know this, because looking back on my own life; they have done this very thing for me.

It's also challenging to let our awesomeness lead us when we have so many thoughts about the things we're not so awesome at. You have two choices moving forward: allow yourself to focus on the good or allow yourself to focus on the bad. It's 100% your choice on what to spend your currency on. Every person on the

64

planet has attributes they want to change. Stop thinking that everyone else is perfect and you're the only person with an improvement list. Transform the bad to good using the exercise I offered in Chapter 3 and you're golden. Or, let it go. If you don't want to change it, at the very least no longer dwell on it. Life is so much easier when you lead with your brilliance. Your perception of yourself in the world is exactly how others will see you.

When I made this change personally, even complete strangers started treating me differently. I noticed that people started looking at me – making eye contact. Babies would smile at me and I would interact back. Elderly people would ask me questions. Women would make small talk in the produce department at the grocery store. I don't really know if this was happening before I made a conscious effort to be aware of the people in my space, but once I changed my perception about leading with my brilliance, my energy shifted and I started being seen – an attribute related to my core childhood wound.

Getting Ready to Get Ready to Get Ready

If you're one of those people who keeps gathering information but not taking action, you're in a perpetual "getting ready" phase. This doesn't actually move you forward. You're probably waiting for the perfect time. Like next week, after that special event. Or, maybe after the holidays have passed. Oh, I know. January 1. That's a great day to start fresh! How many times have you told yourself "I'll start on Monday?" The point is that you're just getting ready to get ready to get ready and you're not actually taking action to move your life forward. When is that time? There is never a perfect time. It's like having a baby. If you wait until you're a specific age, or you have a certain amount of money in savings, or when your career is at a certain level, for example, you will never have a baby. Your circumstances will never be perfect. And if all of the stars happen to align, life may still send you a curve ball, like secondary infertility, something I can absolutely relate to. Your life is happening right now, this very minute you are reading this book. You can put this book down and go back to the life that's keeping you stuck, or you can start implementing everything we've been talking about. It's 100% your choice to stay in a funk, or move yourself forward.

What makes you happy and excited about your future should make you want to jump out of bed every day. It should energize you. It should motivate you to work your corporate job like mad, and come home and spend another full-time day working on your future self. Your family should notice your behavior changes so obviously that they have no option but to take you seriously. That's when you know you are digging down deep to make things happen for yourself. No one will do this for you, and subtlety will not get you there. Take bold action.

Set Your Priorities and Accept the Consequences

No matter your decisions in life, you have the power to set your priorities. When you're in auto-pilot mode, not making intentional decisions, you are still setting your priorities. They will default to where the river wants to pull you downstream. I know this, because I let it happen. If you're not going to control the direction of your boat, then simply accept the consequences of not making intentional decisions. You're probably in a funk because you got in that boat, you didn't steer it, and now you don't want to accept the consequences. Those two don't go very well together. That's the feeling you get when the universe is telling you to make intentional decisions to go in the direction that you want. That feeling is your calling to make different choices. Making decisions allows you to feel in control of your destiny.

Connecting to a Greater Power

The most powerful perception changer for me was my relationship with the universe. Some people refer to God, or spirit, or source, and that's all the same thing to me. I wasn't raised religiously. My parents were different religions themselves and gave me the space to form my own beliefs based on how concepts resonated with my heart. So, I was never baptized as a Christian, which my mom still struggles with to this day. The layers of trauma I experienced distracted me from making a strong connection with God for decades. You might say that the distracting circumstances were the very circumstances I needed this relationship with God for. This was a lonely place. I felt disconnected from everything during many periods. I considered suicide. Ultimately, my strong connection to my son, my whole world, gave me the strength to find my way out from this hopeless place. But, that's not when I started to believe that another energetic realm existed.

My adoptive dad passed away in 2012; we had been estranged for 17 years. Not talking to the person who raised me since I was a baby meant there was a lot of unresolved baggage surrounding this relationship. Needless to say, there were a lot of unsaid words at the time of his death. I tried to extend the olive branch many times over the years, but I never got a response. When he passed, my hope of reconciliation died with him. My biological father, who I had only met twice in my teens, passed away before my adoptive dad in 2006. We had a lot of unsaid words as well. I never really felt like I had a dad in the way I observed my friends' relationships with theirs. It was complicated. I felt a stronger connection to other fathers in my life, but it didn't make me want the relationship any less with my own.

I desperately wanted resolution with these relationships, so I went to a spiritual advisor who a friend recommended. I talked to her about my depression, my lack of belief in God, my fear of death, my feelings of loneliness and brokenness. She was also a medium – someone who could relay messages from people who had passed away. I was interested, but skeptical in this practice, but the day I talked to her my life changed forever. Both of my dads spoke through her to me. Their unique physical appearance and personalities and acknowledgment of their B.S. were present. They were effectively fighting over the phone line to share messages with me. One apologized for not being present in my life at all; acknowledging that he was a hot mess in his life, and said that in spite of him I turned out to be a wonderful person. The other apologized for being arrogant, and mean, and badgering to my mom and me. He acknowledged that my attempts to reach out to school counselors and law enforcement were warranted and that he apologized for lying to cover his own behavior up. They both said they were proud of me, and they always loved me even when it didn't seem like it. Over a period of two years, I saw two more mediums. Both dads came through, in the same way, all three times. These experiences provided me with the information I needed to hear to heal my heart, forgive them for the pain they caused and I finally believed in God.

This was only possible, because I changed my perception about how God works. I opened my heart to see things in a different way; I was open to possibilities.

You can completely change your life when you change your perceptions.

After working with my client Amanda, she told me "I was exactly that person who just let life take me where it wanted because I wasn't paddling in an intentional direction. I have been down for many years because I wasn't sure where to start with getting my life back on track. Vanessa was able to ensure I got through each step of the *Conquering Your Funk* process and answered all of the questions I had when I was stuck. I'm thinking a lot more positively these days and truly believe that I can make my future whatever I want it to be. No more floating down the river for me!"

Chapter 8 –

The Unfunk Toolkit

"If you give people tools, and they use their natural abilities and their curiosity, they will develop things in ways that will surprise you very much beyond what you might have expected." Bill Gates

When you want a short-cut to any of the tools that we've covered in this book, you can refer to this chapter to access them quickly. I've added some bonus tools to help you as well. All of these worksheets are located on my website, https://www.theconfidencespot.com/, as part of "The Unfunk Toolkit: 13 Tools to Help Get You Unfunked" and will help you during your journey.

Tool 1: Writing Your Life Story

This is exactly what it sounds like; write your life story. It doesn't have to be pretty or grammatically correct or in some format presentable to anyone else but you. Start from the beginning, from before you were born even – anything you think has influenced you – and start writing. You can write chronologically. You can write randomly. You can write stories about your life that you remember. Just get it down on paper. You're doing this for you. It is cathartic – healing – to get it all out of your head. Write down how you felt physically; write down your thoughts about it then and your thoughts about it now. Include all of the wonderful things that happened, and all of your accomplishments, and times you felt on top of the world. Write down if you think something is holding you back or dimming your light. Write down what you want to change about it. Write about your hopes and your dreams. Write about your barriers. Just write. Write until you cry, until you just don't have any more to put on paper.

You'll use this information to pull from for the other exercises, so you cannot skip this process; it is foundational to you conquering your funk. Create your God Box (see Tool 2) and store this document there for safe keeping so the universe can honor your story and journey of healing.

Tool 2: God Box

The purpose of a God Box, is to create a sacred place for your written intentions to be held in honor. This box can be anything you want. In fact, it doesn't even need to be a box. It can be a brown paper bag if that's what you have. But, I encourage you to make something beautiful. My God Box started as a white photo box I bought from a local craft store. I wanted the theme to match my office decor, so I painted it silver and Caribbean blue and adorned glittery butterflies on the front and top. That way, it can sit out in the open to remind me to set daily intentions, and honor them.

Not only can you put your written life story in there, you should add messages of desired manifestation to it. Anything you want to attract into your life, you should write a message about it. And, there is a proper way to do it. Remember how I told you that you get exactly what you want from the universe? It's true, and you can really screw this up if you don't manifest it in the correct way. You need to attach an authentic feeling of gratitude or thankfulness or love to your request of the universe. Here is an example:

Don't Say: I want to lose 10 pounds.

You'll Get: More of wanting to lose 10 pounds.

Instead, Say: Thank you, universe, for this slender and healthy body

Don't Say: I want to marry Bob at any cost!

You'll Get: The wrong Bob or you may even get the Bob you want, but maybe it's because his wife dies of cancer and he is widowed, but he is too heartbroken to really love again.

Instead Say: Thank you, universe, for the most fulfilling relationship of my life

Say your desired manifestation as if you are already experiencing what you want. And really mean it. And be very specific. The universe will match your vibration. Raise your vibration, and raise it again. And, if your vibration is disingenuous, the universe will know that too. Regularly add desired manifestations to the box a morning ritual is a great practice. When your God Box fills up, you can burn the papers in a fireplace to honor your intentions.

Tool 3: Charting Your Timeline of Life Changing Events

Take a long piece of paper and draw a line straight across landscape style. This line represents your entire life. The far left hand side shows the year of your birth. The middle of the line shows the current year. The far right hand side shows the date of your 100th birthday.

Draw ticker marks in between to illustrate the years in between. Take your life story, and start plotting when all of those things happened. As you plot, draw a dot on the line and fill it in. Create a corresponding note with the dot so you know what it represents. Once you have everything plotted, go back and make some dots larger based on how impactful you think they have been in your life. Your core wound will be the biggest circle on your timeline (See Tool 4 for help with this). You should have a variety of sizes of dots on your line. The left-hand side of your paper will be filled up with critical events of your past. The right-hand side of your paper will be blank - it is where your intentional future will be created later.

Tool 4: Core Wound/Negative Core Belief Exploration

A professional therapist can really help you identify and heal your core wound effectively. Here's a good place to start learning about this practice in depth and a process I support in my mentoring program:

http://www.aliceboyes.com/cognitive-behavior-therapy-blog-straightforward-guide-to-cbt/

Tool 5: What Are You Awesome At?

Collect all of your thoughts and input from other sources; ask questions about yourself such as:

- What makes you feel proud?
- What comes easy for you that others seem to struggle with?
- What do others ask you for help with because you are the expert or trust your opinion?
- What achievements or awards have you accomplished?
- What has been written about you in your performance reviews?
- What does your family say about you?
- What do your friends say about you?
- What do social groups say about you?
- What knowledge, skills, and abilities do you list on your resume?
- What are your hidden talents that you haven't shown the world   yet?

Tool 6: What Are You Not-So-Awesome At?

Collect all of your thoughts and input from other sources; your list of perceived weaknesses might look like this:

- I am too shy to talk to strangers
- I am not a good writer
- I suck at doing math in my head
- I am not a good manager
- I am too fat to have my picture taken
- I have never been able to share my opinions openly
- I won't ever be able to pass that important test
- I can't earn more than what my current paycheck is
- I am not smart enough to start my own business
- I am too scared to take public transportation
- I am too soft-spoken
- I am terrible at being organized
- I can't multi-task

Tool 7: Reframing Negatives to Positives

Here is an example of the questions to ask yourself about the things you don't think you're so awesome at. Fill in the questions and answers to everything you have listed after completing Tool 6.

1. **I'm not-so-awesome at**: Being a good manager.
2. **Why do I think this?** First, I feel uneasy about being a manager. I am nervous. Also, feedback I have received from my boss and my 360-degree performance review says that my team does not think I am a good manager.
3. **Is this what I think or did someone plant this thought?** Both. I think this about myself and I am being told this.
4. **What am I gaining by thinking this?** Nothing. I continue to act like I am not a good manager because people think I am

not a good manager and I feel like I am not doing a great job. I am going in circles.

5. **Does that belief serve you?** No, continually thinking that I am not a good manager is not making me be a better manager.

6. **Why do you think you think that way?** I didn't really get any training on how to be a manager, let alone how to be a good one. I was promoted because I was good at my job, but I have never led people before. I was just thrown in there. I feel like a fraud.

7. **How could you benefit by not thinking this way?** I would probably be more open to learning how to be a good manager. Right now I am so stuck on how I am not good and that it consumes my confidence.

8. **Is it possible for you start doing the thing that you're not so awesome at, in a way that serves you?** Yes! I can start thinking about this differently. I can start acting the way I think I good manager would ask, and I can go to my boss and let them know I could benefit from some formal management training.

9. **What might be the lesson in the thing you're not-so-awesome at?** Well, maybe this is a lesson that I need to advocate for myself more, in order to be in service of others. I would not have been promoted if my boss didn't see potential in me. And, my boss knew that I didn't have formal management training when I was promoted into the position. Perhaps they are waiting for me to demonstrate leadership skills by asking for help in an area I am weak and they will appreciate my initiative.

Tool 8: Happiness Meditation

Sit quietly and think about something that makes you happy. I mean REALLY happy. Maybe it's puppies. Maybe it's seeing one of your kids do something amazing. Maybe it's something you accomplished that you feel proud of. What does the physical sensation of happiness feel like to you?

Start from the top of your head and work down to your toes, evaluating each part of your body as you scan down acknowledging how happiness makes you feel. Take long, deep breaths as you scan through each part of your body, evaluating your feelings. Close your eyes for a moment and do this. Now, evaluate if your life and work is aligned with this level of happiness feeling. Your life needs to make you feel like you're surrounded in a room with a bunch of puppies every moment of every day.

Tool 9: Envision Your Future

Part 1: Be sure you are in a relaxed state before using this tool. You want to be sure that your energy is open and optimistic, because you'll be declaring what you want your future to be. Write these statements as if you are currently experiencing what you want and answer these questions. Get creative, get detailed, and include all of the stuff you think is too obnoxious (but you really want it anyway).

How do I look? What does my hair look like? What clothing am I wearing? What does my body look like? Do I look relaxed? Do I look excited? Am I smiling?

How do you feel? Are you REALLY happy? Do you feel confident? Do you feel like you are in your element? Do you feel on top of the world?

What are your thoughts? Are you thinking about how awesome you are? Are you funneling your energy into what you're not good at? Are you feeling super confident?

Who are you with? Which people are surrounding you? Who are you spending time with? Are these people supporting you? Are you serving these people with your awesomeness? Is this your current tribe or new people or a mix? How do those people look?

Part 2: Look in the mirror and declare something you want for yourself. Then look back at yourself in the mirror and say "Self, you can have it."

Part 3: Make a daily ritual out of reading your intentions, telling yourself you can have it and adding more specificity and desires each day.

Tool 10: Your Barriers

Building an awareness of your barriers is critical to your success in being able to get out of your funk. If you think you're perfect and don't have anything to change and you're in a funk – that's why you're in a funk. You're probably picking up on the energy the universe is sending back to you with the behaviors you need to change. Sometimes it's hard to recognize for ourselves where we're stuck – what our barriers are – but many times those around us know exactly where we should start. Lead with your brilliance and ask others who know and love you the most where they see you struggling; those are your barriers and are keeping you in a funk.

Part 1: Answer these questions about yourself:

1. What did you learn about your life story?
2. What did you learn about the list of what you're not awesome at?
3. Do you have fears using what you are awesome at to serve the world?
4. What's your health status?
5. How are your relationships with others? Are any strained or broken?
6. What are your bad habits?
7. Who is in your circle of influence?
8. What types of negative thoughts do you have?
9. Where does your lack of happiness come from?
10. What are the B.S. stories you keep telling yourself?
11. Why do you have lack of clarity?

12. Why do you lack taking action?
13. What's your amygdala's role in creating barriers for you?
14. What are false perceptions you have about yourself and others?
15. What are bad assumptions you've made?
16. What is your parental programming?
17. What trauma haven't you dealt with?
18. What habits can you change? Both productive and non-productive?
19. How can you start to advocate for your health?
20. What is your money shit? In paper and thought form?
21. Are you projecting your B.S. on other people?

Part 2: Rank each answer based on what you think is causing the greatest agony in your life right now (1-Most Agony, 21-Least Agony).

Part 3: Take a look at the item you ranked as #1; that is what you will start working on improving.

Tool 11: Perceptions as a Way of Being

Begin moving your thoughts and actions in an intentional way towards what you want and how you want things to be. Do not spend your thoughts and actions on what you do not want. Stop yourself when you begin to think negatively, or spend your thought currency on anything other than what you desire.

Tool 12: Make Lasting Changes via Macro and Micro goals

Here's an example about how to set Macro and Micro goals: Say you smoke 7 cigarettes per day and your goal is to quit altogether. Today, just commit to smoke 6 cigarettes per day for 21 days. On day 22, reduce to 5 cigarettes per day, and so on. If you slip up, simply stay on the Micro goal that you're having trouble with for another round until you master it, then start reducing again. You can apply this to things you want to start doing more of as well, such as drinking more water or exercising. The sky is the limit with ideas this will work for.

Tool 13: Goal Setting

If you're a person who likes setting goals in a visual way, I can totally relate. I have a goal board in my office that I list mine on and update them weekly. Much of what I do personally involves butterflies – it's my spirit animal and my namesake – so naturally I made my goal board follow suit. I simply bought a framed chalk board at a local hobby store and painted the frame silver to match my office. I used colored chalk to write my goals and glued more of those glittery butterflies to the frame (it matches my God Box!). The title of my goal board says "Operation Metamorphosis" because my goal setting relates to my personal transformation about the intentions I am setting for my life. The various stages of metamorphosis represent the various stages of my goals. On the far left-hand side, I have listed "The Egg" – this is the column that my overarching goal is written, such as "Book." The next column over is "Larva" – this column represents the next phase in the goal process, which is listed as "Finalize manuscript." The next column over is "Goal Date" – which represents when this goal needs to be achieved. The next column over is "Chrysalis" – this is the column that represents the next stage, which represents the next step of my goal (this goal will move into the "Larva" column when the previous goal has been met) – it's listed as "Receive Manuscript Feedback from Publisher." The next column over is "Adult" – this column represents the final form, the ultimate goal, which is listed as "Published Book." The final column is named "Metamorphosis Date", which represents the date the goal will have fully materialized, which is listed as "January 2017." Get "The Unfunk Toolkit" from https://www.theconfidencespot.com/ for a visual of this.

Conclusion

Your Path to Funk Freedom

"Our deepest fear is not that we are inadequate. Our deepest fear is that we are powerful beyond measure. It is our light, not our darkness that most frightens us. We ask ourselves, Who am I to be brilliant, gorgeous talented, fabulous? Actually, who are you not to be? Your playing small does not serve the world. There is nothing enlightened about shrinking so that other people won't feel insecure around you. We are all meant to shine, as children do." Marianne Williamson

Start to Paddle

You're already in the boat, but when are you going to start paddling in the direction you want to go? Time is going to pass, regardless of you taking action. But, do you want to come to your senses in a year from now wishing that you had just started today? Chances are, you already did that last year, and the year before or maybe even a decade ago. There is a reason why you bought this book. Your funk is getting the best of you and you are ready to lead with your brilliance and banish your B.S. Your funk might be telling you that you aren't strong enough to paddle. But, you are. You have it within you to start paddling TODAY.

What are You Waiting for Exactly?

Are you getting ready to get ready to get ready? Probably. That's why you've been stuck in a funk. You have all of the tools to help you uncover the information you need to start moving forward today. If you've done the exercises as we've moved through the book, you have a treasure trove of information to help heal your heart and let your light start to shine.

- You documented your life story
- You have a handle on where you came from and how it influenced you
- You MORPHed yourself, looking at five critical areas of your life:
  o Mental Well-being
  o Our World
  o Relationships
  o Personal Habits
  o Healthy Living
- You declared what you're awesome at so you can lead with your brilliance
- You acknowledged what you're not so awesome at and how you can use it to your advantage
- You tapped into feelings to help you identify what makes you really happy
- You envisioned your intentional future
- You worked through all of the barriers that you think are holding you back
- You identified how all of this is holding you back at work, in your career, and maybe you want a total re-do to start playing BIG
- You have begun conquering your funk by:
  o Unfunking your brilliance
  o Unfunking your weakness
  o Unfunking your happiness
  o Unfunking your barriers

80

o Unfunking your future

Most importantly, you learned that you are 100% in control of changing the direction of your life, by the way you think about your circumstances, by the intentions you make and by the actions you take.

After following my program, my client Maggie said "What an intensive process this program has been! I have learned so much about myself and was able to connect the dots about why I behave a certain way based on how I was raised. I was having a hard time at work prior to working through these issues, but since making an intentional shift in how I wanted to be seen, my boss noticed a huge difference and my most recent performance review has been the best one yet!"

What Path Will You Take Now?

Listen, I shared a ton of really personal stories with you to illustrate how I conquered my funk. If I can do it, so can you. I've given you all of the short-cuts to my success. But, I do understand that trying to conquer your funk might be daunting to do it alone. You might not know where to start or how to use the tools that I've described. You might not feel like you have the tribe to support you along the way. I totally understand.

That's exactly why I started mentoring women who are just like you – a program that follows the outline of this book, and goes deeper into the topics we've discussed here in a more intimate way. A way where you can build connection with other women who want to live the life they are meant to live. Women who want to lead with their brilliance and banish their B.S. Women who want to start paddling the boat in the direction they want to go instead of the direction life happens to take them. Women who are done with the mediocre life of playing small, and those who are done letting barriers get the best of them. Women like you.

When are you going to start playing big? When are you going to come out of the darkness and shine your brilliance and let the world see your gifts – your authentic self? My hope is that you have already started during the course of reading this book.

If you want a new tribe of supportive women who want exactly what you want, guided by a leader who has created the path for you by already walking it, I would love for you to join us.

Your Personalized Path Awaits

If you'd like to work with me, head over to my website at https://www.theconfidencespot.com/ and check out the various ways you can work with me!

May you lead with your brilliance!

Further Reading

The Law of Divine Compensation by Marianne Williamson

Feelings Buried Alive Never Die by Karol K. Truman

How to Get What You Really, Really, Really, Really Want by Dr. Wayne Dyer and Deepak Chopra, M.D.

Mind Over Mood by Dennis Greenberger, Ph. D. and Christine A. Pedesky

Now, Discover Your Strengths by Marcus Buckingham & Donald O. Clifton, Ph.D.

Tears to Triumph by Marianne Williamson

The Body Keeps the Score by Bessel Van Der Kolk, M.D.

The Game of Life and How to Play It by Florence Scovel Shinn

The ACEs Revolution! The Impact of Adverse Childhood Experiences by John Richard Traysner

The Happiness Project by Gretchen Rubin

The Law of Attraction by Esther and Jerry Hicks

Total Money Makeover by Dave Ramsey

You Are a Badass, How to Stop Doubting Your Greatness and Start Living an Awesome Life by Jen Sincero

Acknowledgements

My personal transformation would not have been possible had it not been for my friends and family.

Thank you, to my son, Kegan as my path was uncertain until the day you were born. You gave me the focus that I lacked as a nineteen-year-old single mother. You were a lesson in love that I needed so badly. You taught me to dig down deep to fight the hard battles; failure wasn't an option for us. You have been my best friend for 20 years. Thank you for inspiring me every day to keep moving forward, even in the dark days when I wanted to quit and give up. You can still read me like no one else. You have been my guiding light.

Thank you, to my husband, Tres. You give me a sense of peace, a feeling that used to be hard to come by. Your strength and wisdom counsel me. Your confidence is contagious. You are kind, gentle, and honest. I never question that you love me, my son, and my absurd number of pets, with all you have. I love you more than all of the stars in the universe. Thank you for taking this journey with me, and believing in me.

Thank you, to my mother, Lorie. Without you, I would not be on this earth. You showed me how to be kind and thoughtful, and the importance of gratitude. You demonstrated a work ethic to be rivaled. Your strength and perseverance are attributes I admire. Your love for me has been unwavering. Sadly, I did not pick up your cooking, baking, or sewing skills. Thank you for cheering me on, no matter what. Thank you for giving me the courage to share my journey openly so I can help others. I love you more.

Thank you, to my closest friends over the years, Brigette, Cindy, Lucinda, Joanne, and Angie. You know all the stories. Thank you for listening to my gripes and my struggles, and helping where you could. You babysat, you gave me grocery money, you tutored me in statistics, you were the call when I needed to escape from terrible dates, you gave me an ear and a shoulder to cry on. You were my emergency contacts and my references. You gave me a friend when I felt alone. You gave me the encouragement to keep working toward my dreams. No matter how far apart we are, you have always been by my side. Collectively, you are my unwavering cheering section.

Thank you, to my mentor and friend, Lynnette. You believed in me at age 19. You gave me unreasonable responsibility, and I thrived. You made sure that I had a computer at home to write my college papers so I didn't have to stay away from my baby to type them after work. Thank you for seeing the potential and giving me a chance. Your mentorship paved a successful path for me for which I will be forever grateful.

Thank you, to Charlie and Diane. You didn't need to accept me into your life when your grandson was born, but you did without reservation. Thank you for allowing me to join your family and have a place at the table for the last 20 years. Your support means more to me than you will ever know and I cannot imagine how life would have been without your family.

Thank you, to my 2016 health-care team. You saw the hope in my case. You saw small, incremental changes as possibilities for a transformational recovery.

About the Author

Vanessa Newport is the world's only funk-fixing-confidence-catapulting catalyst and leads her mentorship clients through a process of healing and self-discovery, allowing them to get out of their funk and emerge inspired to lead with their brilliance and banish their B.S. Her tenacious approach to tackling life's challenges lead to healing and hope and a mission to help others. Vanessa loves speaking and sharing her passion about women living with intention at home and at work. She enjoys getting to know people, traveling, is a novice photographer and has an affinity for alpacas. Vanessa's background includes over 20 years in the Human Resources field, with certifications from the Society of Human Resources Management, Human Resources Certification Institute and International Foundation of Employee Benefit Plans. Vanessa lives in Aurora, CO, with her husband, son, and an absurd number of pets.

Vanessa can be reached through various social media platforms listed on her website, https://www.theconfidencespot.com.

Thank You

My sincere gratitude for allowing me the opportunity to share my story with you!

COMPLIMENTARY TOOLKIT!

I've created "The Unfunk Toolkit" as a companion to this book at https://www.theconfidencespot.com/.

READY FOR MENTORSHIP?

Head over to my website at https://www.theconfidencespot.com to check out the variety of ways to work with me.

JOIN MY TRIBE!

Engage in the conversation to learn how to unfunk and flourish!

I can be reached on various social media platforms from my website at https://www.theconfidencespot.com.

Made in the USA
San Bernardino, CA
12 February 2018